The Horse Rider's Handbook

Monty Mortimer

David & Charles

Other titles in *The Equestrian Library* series:

THE HORSE OWNER'S HANDBOOK
Monty Mortimer

KEEPING A HORSE OUTDOORS
Susan McBane

LUNGEING THE HORSE AND RIDER
Sheila Inderwick

A DAVID & CHARLES BOOK

First published in the UK in 1989
Reprinted 1989, 1992
First published in paperback 2003

Copyright © Monty Mortimer 1989, 2003

Distributed in North America
by F&W Publications, Inc.
4700 East Galbraith Road
Cincinnati, OH 45236
1-800-289-0963

Printed in Great Britain by Antony Rowe Ltd
for David & Charles
Brunel House   Newton Abbot   Devon

Visit our website at www.davidandcharles.co.uk

David & Charles books are available from all good bookshops;
alternatively you can contact our Orderline on (0)1626 334555 or write to us
at FREEPOST EX2 110, David & Charles Direct, Newton Abbot, TQ12 4ZZ
(no stamp required UK mainland).

Contents

Introduction

Until the advent of the internal combustion engine, man's progress towards civilisation was borne on the back of the horse. This willing animal fought his wars, tilled his land, carried his load, pulled his cart and powered his early machinery. Now that horse power has been replaced by fossil fuels and nuclear power man's interest in the horse is largely in the pursuit of sport and leisure.

The present-day equine manifests himself in so many breeds, types and varieties that he lends himself to a wide range of very diverse sporting activities. The ponies alone range from the Shetland on which small children can be taught through the various native breeds, to the hard, strong polo pony that can stand the rigours of high goal polo. The horse is equally versatile, ranging from the heavyweight Clydesdale through the hack, hunter and cob to the sleek thoroughbred racehorse.

Whatever purpose the ridden horse is put to, it should be remembered that he was not designed as a carrier, he is much better suited to pulling. The rider sits almost in the weakest part of the horse's back, just in front of the loins and presents the horse with a top-heavy load, unbalancing his natural equilibrium. The draught horse, however, when fitted with a collar or breast girth can throw his great weight against the load and pull with his powerful muscles.

To obtain the best results from the horse it is important that the rider is proficient in three distinct but closely related areas. Firstly he must develop his riding skill to enable him to ride efficiently. Secondly he must understand the psychology of the horse and thirdly the rider must have a detailed knowledge of the animal's anatomy and physiology. Without a comprehensive knowledge in these areas the rider will limit his ability to get the best from his horse.

No matter which of the equestrian disciplines is to be followed, these basic requirements remain the same. Once they are understood the challenges of competition riding are much easier to accomplish. It is these skills and the various sporting challenges that this book is concerned with.

1 The Horse

Psychology

The ability to understand how the horse reacts to various conditions is a most important part of training and riding. Without a knowledge of the psychology of the horse there is a danger that the trainer or rider will attempt to dominate the horse by physical force which almost certainly results in physical and mental damage to the animal. This must detract from the relationship between the horse and rider and prevent a true partnership being formed. The rider who understands the way that the horse reacts to various conditions will be able to mould tactfully the horse's responses to his advantage, taking him into his confidence as a partner rather than as an opponent.

Natural instincts

The horse has a number of basic, natural instincts that govern and control his life. These instincts may prove to be to the rider's advantage or disadvantage. In some instances they may prove to be both.

The natural reaction that most affects the training of the horse is his ability and willingness to get up onto his toes and run. Without these qualities the horse would not be suitable for many of the activities for which he is used. The racehorse that does not have the desire to run would be useless, this would apply equally well to the hunter, show jumper, polo pony or gymkhana pony. Until this willingness to run is controlled, and the horse understands how and when his power is to be used, the horse is difficult to ride.

The horse's first line of defence when he is hurt or frightened is to run away. He has no teeth like the canines, claws like the felines nor horns like the antelopes with which to defend himself so his immediate reaction to danger is to run. If you go into a field that contains a mixture of horses and cattle and alarm them, the cattle will turn towards you and lower their heads in a threatening manner. The horses, on the other hand, will run away to a safe distance then turn around to look at you. The horse will only resort to his hooves or his teeth as a means of defence when he is cornered. If a groom enters the stable without letting the horse know that he is coming and alarms him, he may well kick out with a hind foot. If, before mounting, the rider abruptly tightens the girth, pinching the skin, the horse may respond by nipping the rider with his teeth. Neither the teeth nor the hind feet are natural defences for the horse, they are only used in circumstances where escape is impossible.

The next most basic instinct in the horse that affects his behaviour and training is the herd instinct. He likes the security of being in a herd with his fellows and only after considerable, tactful training will the horse be willing to work on his own away from the herd. This very strong instinct may create problems when riding as the horse may be unwilling to leave the collecting ring at a show or, when out hunting, be unwilling to leave the field and go off on his own. On the other hand, it is often an advantage to train the young horse with other older and more experienced horses in the hope that he will copy their behaviour.

The horse that is reluctant to jump a fence may well follow a more experienced jumper over it when given a lead. When designing a show-jumping course for a novice competition the course builder may well face the first jump towards the collecting ring to encourage the inexperienced horse to jump towards his fellows and so get him started on the course.

The horse's natural desire to eat can also be used to the rider's advantage. The horse that is difficult to catch in the field can often be tempted by a few oats or horse cubes in a bucket as can the horse that is unwilling to load into a trailer or horse box. A haynet is often given to a horse to pacify him whilst he is being clipped or shod. The food distracts him whilst these unnatural activities are being carried out.

In some equestrain disciplines the stallion is at an advantage over the castrated male. His elegance and high courage are often an advantage in dressage. In racing the successful stallion can pass on his qualities to his progeny. In other disciplines however, the stallion is at a disadvantage in that his attention and discipline may be lost in the presence of mares.

The horse does best in quiet surroundings free from noise and excitement. In general, the quiet, tactful horse handler is more successful than one of an excitable disposition.

Much can be ascertained from the horse by his stance and attitude. It is good that he should lie down as this usually denotes that he feels secure and relaxed. The horse that lies down looking distressed or awkward may be indicating that all is not well. The horse that paces continually round his box or up and down the fence of his field is indicating that something is wrong as is the horse that crib bites or wind sucks. A lot can be learnt from the attitude of the ears. When at rest they should be relaxed but mobile. The ears are pricked when the horse is alert and focussing on one object with both eyes. When they are laid flat down his neck he is distressed, tense or angry. The tail of the contented horse should be relaxed and lie centrally between the buttocks. The tense, clamped down or crooked tail is a sign of distress or tension as is the tail that is swished from side to side or round in circles. The tail that is held high, sometimes almost erect, is a sign of excitement often shown by the high stepping stallion when turned out in a field of mares.

The association of ideas is an important part of all animal training. Much of the horse's training is brought about by reward for doing well and reprimand for doing badly. The horse will respond to a pat on the neck and a congratulatory word when he does well. He will also learn that a slap with the whip behind the saddle is an indication that he has done something wrong. The timing of these congratulations or admonitions is, however, important. The pat on the neck should coincide, as much as possible, with the act that has prompted it as must the admonition accompany the error. If the horse bites the groom whilst being brushed in the stable, it is no use giving the horse a slap five minutes later. The whip must be kept handy so that the next nip can be accompanied by a sharp slap

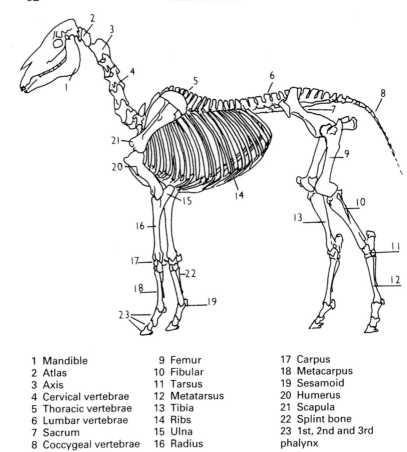

1 Mandible	9 Femur	17 Carpus
2 Atlas	10 Fibular	18 Metacarpus
3 Axis	11 Tarsus	19 Sesamoid
4 Cervical vertebrae	12 Metatarsus	20 Humerus
5 Thoracic vertebrae	13 Tibia	21 Scapula
6 Lumbar vertebrae	14 Ribs	22 Splint bone
7 Sacrum	15 Ulna	23 1st, 2nd and 3rd
8 Coccygeal vertebrae	16 Radius	phalynx

Fig 1 The horse's skeleton

from the groom. The horse will then associate the slap with nipping and learn not to do it.

Anatomy and Physiology
The anatomy and physiology of the horse is an extensive and complex subject but without a basic knowledge of the way in which the animal functions the rider or trainer will limit his ability to get the best from his horse.

This brief study of the subject will show in simple terms how the horse's skeleton, muscle structure, digestive system, blood circulation and respiratory system work and how they should be taken into consideration when riding and training the horse.

The skeleton

As in all vertebrates the skeleton is the framework consisting of bone and cartilage that supports the muscles and all the organs that make up the complete animal. It is a masterpiece of engineering and enables the horse, by the actions of his muscles, to propel himself forwards, upwards, sideways and backwards through all his natural paces.

The skeleton consists of four main parts: the head and neck; the main body consisting of the spine, rib-cage and pelvis; four legs and a tail.

The head and the neck consist of the skull and seven

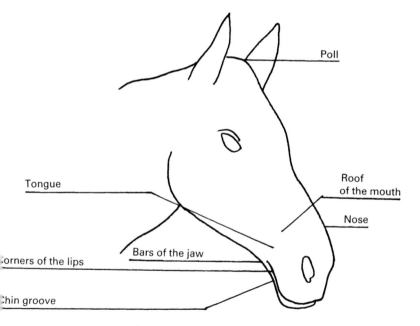

Fig 2 The areas of the horse's head on which the bit and bridle have an effect

cervical vertebrae. The head and the neck, in addition to containing vital organs such as the brain, eyes, ears and facilities for breathing and eating, play a considerable part in the horse's balance. In all his locomotion the head and neck are used as a sort of balancing pole to help to maintain his equilibrium. This is why the size of the head, the length of the neck and the way in which they are attached to one another are so important in overall conformation.

The spine is the mainstay of the whole body structure providing a frame for the attachment of the legs for locomotion, the ribs which enclose the major organs of the body and the vital neck and head. There are eighteen thoracic vertebrae with a pair of ribs attached to each, six lumbar vertebrae and a sacrum consisting of five bones fused together. The horse's pelvis consists of the hip bone, the sacrum and the first three coccygeal vertebrae.

There are eighteen pairs of ribs. The eight pairs at the front of the chest are attached to the thoracic vertebrae and extend to join the sternum. These are sometimes known as 'true' ribs. The ten ribs to the rear are not attached to the sternum but are joined by cartilage. These are known as 'false' ribs. The rib-cage protects the vital internal organs: it also, by muscular action, plays a major role in breathing. Expansion of the rib cage encourages the inflow of air into the lungs. In turn muscular contraction of the rib-cage expels air from the lungs.

Unlike the greyhound, cheetah or other galloping animals, the horse is handicapped by an almost total absence of flexibility in the spine. This means that he is unable to arch his back and bring his hind legs really underneath his body as the greyhound would do. It is sometimes said that '. . . the horse, when circling, should bend throughout the length of his body on the circumference of the circle.' An examination of the skinned cadaver of the horse will show that there is virtually no lateral flexion through the rib-cage. The legs support and propel the horse. In spite of their apparently frail construction they are immensely strong, being able to carry not only the weight of the horse but also the weight of a rider with saddle and bridle. The horse was never designed as a load-carrying animal and a purely superficial examination of his body will show how totally unsuitable he is for this task. Nevertheless his great courage, adaptability and co-operative nature have combined to overcome the disadvantages of his physique.

The hind legs consists of:

1 The femur joining the pelvis to the stifle joint.
2 The stifle joint which is the equivalent of the human knee.
3 The tibia and fibula, joining the stifle to the hock joint.
4 The hock joint, consisting of a number of small bones and corresponding to the human ankle joint.
5 The large metartarsal or cannon bone, connecting the hock and fetlock joints.
6 The phalanges, of which there are three, the long pastern, the short pastern and the pedal or coffin bone.

The hind leg, activated by the great muscles of the hindquarters, propels the horse forward. He is a heavy animal, seldom less than 500kg (1,100lb) with considerable bulk and little or no streamlining. With the addition of the rider's weight and the unnatural work that the riding horse is required to do on surfaces for which he was not designed, these limbs are put under considerable strain. Concussion is less of a problem in the hind limb than in the fore limb, much of it being taken up in the hock joint and the cartilage cushions in the spine. The fetlock, hock and stifle joints are put under considerable strain through flexion, wrenching (turning in deep going), galloping and jumping. This strain can, of course, be minimised by careful training, preparation and shoeing. The fetlock joint in the hind leg is subject to strain, and this will show in the well-worn horse in general puffiness and wind galls. The hock joint is probably the most vital and most abused joint and suffers in similar ways. Ill-conformed hocks, those that are too straight 'cow' or 'sickle' hocks or those with a tendency to curbs, are unlikely to stand up to sustained wear and tear. Strain in the hock joint manifests itself in the form of curbs, spavins and thoroughpins. The stifle joint in the horse corresponds to the human knee joint. It operates in conjunction with the hock joint, the two always flexing together. It is the ability of these two joints to flex that allows the horse to walk, trot, canter or gallop. No matter how much flexion there is in these two joints, unlike the dog or the cat, the horse cannot put his hind foot on the ground further forward than his navel.

The foreleg is the anatomical feature of the horse which is likely to cause more problems than any other. For the work that it is required to do and the strain that it is required to bear, its construction can only be described as frail. Unlike the human the horse has no collar bone which means that the scapula is not attached to the skeleton by a bony connection. It is connected only by muscle and ligaments. As many of the problems found in the foreleg are caused by concussion, this lack of a bony attachment of the foreleg to the rest of the frame may be considered as an advantage. The muscle and ligamentous attachment relieves some of the concussion that would otherwise be passed on to the spine through a connecting bone.

The foreleg consists of the following:

1 The scapula, the equivalent of the human shoulder-blade.
2 The humerus, joining the scapula to the elbow.
3 The radius and the ulna are fused to form one bone in the horse and join the elbow to the knee.
4 The carpus, the seven bones that make up the knee joint.
5 The metacarpal bone or the cannon bone. The splint bones, found at the top and on either side of the cannon bone are the vestigial remains of two digits that were present in the prehistoric horse.
6 The phalanges or the long and short pastern bones and the pedal or coffin bone. These form part of the foot and are connected to the leg by means of the fetlock joint. In close connection are the navicular and two sesamoid bones. Their function is to guide the tendons that operate the limb but they are of particular significance to the rider as they are potential seats of very common, serious injury.

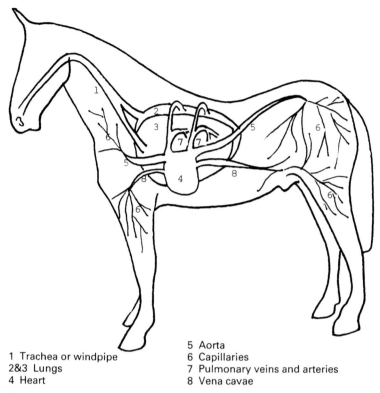

1 Trachea or windpipe	5 Aorta
2&3 Lungs	6 Capillaries
4 Heart	7 Pulmonary veins and arteries
	8 Vena cavae

Fig 3 A diagrammatic view of the circulatory system

Whilst most of the driving power of the horse is provided by the hind legs, a certain amount is produced by
the forelegs. Their prime function, however, is to support
the front of the horse. Very basically, the horse propels
himself by throwing his body forward by thrust from the
hind legs, catching and supporting himself on a foreleg.
It is obvious, particularly when cantering, galloping or
jumping, that the entire weight of the horse and rider
is at some stage in each and every stride supported on
one foreleg, with the pastern joint extended to a greater
or lesser degree. The structure of the foreleg is put under
continuous, considerable strain.
The tail is made up of approximately eighteen coccygeal

vertebrae. A well-formed tail not only enhances the horse's appearance, but it is an indication as to his well-being and mental attitude.

The circulatory system
The purpose of the circulatory system is to pump blood around the body, transporting nutrients and oxygen to the tissues and carrying away waste products.

Blood is composed of plasma, red and white corpuscles and platelets. Plasma is a straw-coloured fluid in which the corpuscles and the platelets float. It transports nourishment (in solution) which has been extracted from food. It also collects waste material and excretes it from the body via the kidneys and skin. Red corpuscles carry oxygen from the lungs to the body tissues. They also transport carbon dioxide from the body tissues to the lungs where it is exhaled. The purpose of the white corpuscles is to maintain health by destroying disease organisms in the blood and tissues. They are outnumbered by red corpuscles by about 500 to 1. Platelets cause blood to congeal and help to seal wounds.

The heart is a pump which in the healthy horse pumps about 36–42 times a minute. It is divided into four main chambers: the right ventricle; the left ventricle; the right auricle and the left auricle. Blood is circulated around the body through arteries, capillaries and veins.

Oxygenated blood is pumped from the left ventricle into the main artery, the aorta. This vessel subdivides until the extremities of the body are reached by capillaries. These are microscopic tubes which connect arteries to veins via the tissues of the body. They have very thin walls through which nutrients and oxygen pass into the cells that make up the body tissues. The capillaries also evacuate waste materials from the tissues.

De-oxygenated blood, dark red in colour, passes from the capillaries into the veins which transport it back to the heart. It enters the right auricle and passes through a valve into the right ventricle. The blood then passes through the pulmonary arteries to the lungs where it is reoxygenated and returned to the left auricle of the heart via the pulmonary veins. From there the refreshed blood is passed to the left ventricle to start circulating again.

The respiratory system

To enable the horse to cope with the unnatural strains that are put upon him when he is ridden he requires an efficient means of inhaling oxygen and exhaling carbon dioxide. He is equipped with a good pair of lungs that work like bellows. They are contained in the chest behind the ribs and operated by the diaphragm. As the rib-cage is expanded the internal pressure is reduced and air enters the lungs. The horse inhales through the nostrils and the air passes through the windpipe or trachea. This divides into two bronchi, one of which goes to each lung. The bronchi subdivide within the lung into bronchial tubes which further subdivide until they end in minute air-sacs or alveoli. Oxygen passes through the thin walls of the aveoli into the blood vessels of the lungs and hence through the pulmonary blood system, via the heart, to the body tissues. De-oxygenated blood is then returned to the lungs where carbon dioxide is extracted and exhaled.

The central nervous system

The central nervous system consists of the brain, which is contained in the skull, and the spinal cord which runs down the centre of the spine.

The brain has two main divisions, the cerebrum, which is the large front part of the brain and the cerebellum which is the smaller, lower part at the back of the skull.

Nerves are a complicated system of links between the brain and the various parts of the body. Motor nerves take messages from the brain and spinal cord to operate muscles and move the limbs. Sensory nerves are receptors in tissues and inform the brain and spinal cord about temperature, pain and sensation.

Body movements are not all controlled by the brain, some are brought about by self-governing or autonomic nerves. These control the continuous body functions that are necessary to support life, such as the heartbeat, breathing, digestion and the many other complex functions of the body and its organs.

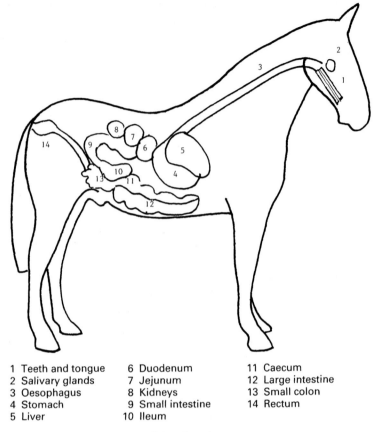

1 Teeth and tongue   6 Duodenum   11 Caecum
2 Salivary glands   7 Jejunum   12 Large intestine
3 Oesophagus   8 Kidneys   13 Small colon
4 Stomach   9 Small intestine   14 Rectum
5 Liver   10 Ileum

Fig 4 A diagrammatic view of the digestive system

The composition of body cells
The horse's body is made up of millions of living cells. A
cell consists of a nucleus supported by protoplasm which is
contained within the cell membrane. The cell is controlled
by the nucleus which dictates its character and establishes
the work that it is to do. Protoplasm is a colourless jelly
maintained within the very thin semi-permeable membrane
of the cell. Food and oxygen pass into the cell through this
membrane and waste products pass out.

   Cells die and are replaced. Skin cells are replaced in a few days, others can live for weeks or months. The exceptions are nerve cells which, once destroyed, are not replaced. Each type of cell has its own particular task, those of the pancreas secrete insulin, for instance, which controls the level of sugar in the blood.

The digestive system

The horse is a grazing animal and has a natural digestive system that is designed to take in and process large quantities of cellulose on a regular and fairly continuous basis. This is because, in his natural habitat, he will graze most of the day. When he is domesticated and fed a diet that will give him sufficient nourishment to be able to work whilst carrying a rider, the natural digestive system must adapt, to be able to cope with the change in circumstances. He requires considerable help from his master if he is to make this adaptation successfully.

Digestion is the breakdown of foodstuffs, such as carbohydrates ingested by the horse, by the action of enzymes to simpler compounds such as glucose and fructose which may then be used in metabolism.

Food is taken into the mouth by the lips and the incisor teeth. It is masticated by the molar teeth which break up the food and mix it with saliva in the mouth. The enzymes in saliva start the digestive process. The tongue and teeth then convert the masticated food into a bolas which is passed into the oesophagus.

In the oesophagus a muscular action, known as the peristaltic wave, carries the bolas through the cardiac sphincter into the stomach. Here the food is mixed with gastric juices by muscular contractions of the stomach wall. The proteins are acted upon by enzymes and converted into peptones. The food is now a soft mash called 'chyme'. It is passed out of the stomach via the pyloric sphincter into the duodenum.

In the duodenum the chyme is acted upon by the liver bile and juices from the pancreas. The enzymes in these fluids break down the chyme further. From the duodenum the chyme passes into the small intestine where digestion continues. Carbohydrates are broken down into glucose and fructose, proteins and peptones are broken down into amino acids and fats become fatty acids. Digestion is completed in the ileum where these nutrients are absorbed through the villi which line its corrugated walls and are passed via the portal vein to the liver.

The residue passes into the large colon or large intestine which is divided into four areas: the right ventral colon; the left ventral colon; the right dorsal colon and the left dorsal colon. The large colon is some twenty-five feet long and it is in this organ that water is absorbed by the bloodstream. The indigestible remains are passed on to the small colon where they accumulate before being expelled via the rectum as faeces.

In the kidneys, waste amino acids in excess of the body's requirements are excreted as urea and expelled in water via the bladder as urine.

Historical Development

In terms of the history of the world the horse, like man, is a comparative newcomer. The earliest fossil remains of the horse's ancestors are only 55 million years old, whereas the dinosaurs became extinct about 65 million years ago, and some rocks have been dated at 5 billion years old.

Fortunately the fossil remains of the horse throughout his evolution are plentiful and complete providing a clear record of his progress over the past 55 million years. The course of equine evolution has not followed a single path. It has taken diverse routes resulting in many breeds and types of horses and ponies together with zebras and asses.

It is certain that the horse first developed in what is now North America and ranged from there to the rest of the world. A few thousand years ago he became extinct in that country but was reintroduced by the sixteenth-century settlers and once again flourished.

The major structural changes that occurred in this animal, and which brought about the present-day horse, were his height, his teeth and the structure of his feet. There were other changes which, whilst important, were less significant.

Hyracotherium or Eophippus existed 55 million years

ago and was the earliest, traceable ancestor of the modern horse. He was about 30cm (12in) tall, his teeth were suitable for eating succulent leaves, his forefeet consisted of a weight-bearing central pad and three hooved toes. As a small browsing animal he became easy prey to larger carnivores. Being without sharp teeth, horns or claws to defend himself his only means of defence was flight. This encouraged Hyracotherium to get up off his flat feet and on to his toes.

Fossil remains from 35 million years ago show a larger animal 60cm (24in) high with similar dentition to Hyracotherium but with one central weight-bearing pad and three hooved toes on each of his four feet. This animal is known as Mesohippus.

The next clear stage in the evolution of the horse is 25 million years ago with the discovery of Merychippus. Now 1m (40in) high he had developed teeth suitable for grazing, and his feet consisted of one load-bearing pad and two side toes.

Plyohippus lived 10 million years ago and was the next stage of development. Now 12 hands high, he had one central hooved toe and the side toes had receded to what we know today as splint bones.

The first evidence of Equus or the present-day horse is found in fossil remains of one million years ago. The horse had developed into the varied type we know today and has been bred up to the excellent standard necessary to succeed in contemporary competitions.

2 The Rider

People who ride horses fall into two very broad categories. Those who use the horse as a means of transport and enjoy hacking out around the countryside or going for a gallop along the beach and those who are sufficiently enthusiastic to want to ride the horse in the most efficient way and to improve him. There is no disgrace in belonging to the first of these two categories, many people derive a great deal of enjoyment from this pastime. It is however the second category that is to be considered here, the rider who wishes to get the very best from his horse, easing his task, improving his work and consequently prolonging his useful life.

Until the end of the nineteenth century the rider's position, in all aspects of horsemanship, was a deep seat, leaning back and with a long stirrup. This was certainly the cavalry seat and that employed by the huntsman and racing jockey. It was usually combined with long spurs and a severe bit which had long cheeks. It was a relic of the equestrian seat taught initially by Xenaphon from 400 BC and the Italian classical schools of the Middle Ages.

It was not until the end of the nineteenth and the beginning of the twentieth centuries that this style was to change. The American jockey Tod Sloan was the first rider to introduce the short stirrup to Britain. In the early 1900s he set new records on most racecourses riding with, what was then, a very short stirrup. His efforts were treated with derision as it was said that: 'He rode like a monkey up a stick.'

At the same time a further equestrian revolution was taking place in Italy. At the Italian cavalry school, at Tor di Quinto, Captain Federico Caprilli, a riding instructor, was to have the most dramatic effect on riding of all time. He was described in his officer cadet reports as a 'less than moderate horseman', but in his tragically short career he was to prove these reports to be quite wrong. Caprilli saw how inefficient and wasteful it was to ride horses across country in the accepted style. He was appalled by the suffering that was inflicted on horses when they were ridden in the old-fashioned way. He developed a style of riding that was to give the horse much greater freedom of his head, neck and back when carrying a rider. He forbade bits with long cheeks and would not allow the trot to be ridden sitting. He insisted that the rider should go forward with his horse whether on the flat, up or downhill or over a jump. This was to bring the centre of gravity of both the horse and the rider closer together and to give the horse greater use of his body in a natural way. To enable the rider to get the top part of his body forward it was necessary to shorten the stirrups which was what Tod Sloan had discovered on the racecourse a few years previously.

Soon the entire Italian cavalry school was riding in this style and Caprilli and his riders were winning at international shows throughout Europe. This resulted in students from British, American, Russian and other cavalry schools flocking to Italy for training. The 'Italian' or 'forward seat' was to spread rapidly around the world. Unfortunately Caprilli was to die as a young man and it appears that his character and intellect were such that his theories were never chronicled. The only records left are those of his disciple and friend Piero Santini and these are only in note form.

It is the forward seat that forms the basis of general-purpose riding today.

Mental Attitude

Riding a horse is a partnership between horse and rider where both are striving for a common aim. Little good ever came from the horse and rider combination in which the rider was on one side against the horse and the course on the other.

The successful rider must truly like the horse. The word 'love' in this respect is over-used and inappropriate. A healthy respect for the horse, together with a thorough knowledge of how he works and thinks, combined with serious devotion to his well-being is what is required.

It appears that some people are born with a natural affinity towards the horse. These people and their horses are comfortable in one another's presence, they ride and handle horses in a relaxed and easy manner. There are those who, in time and with dedication, develop these skills and this attitude but there are also those whose riding and attitude towards the horse appears to remain antagonistic.

Single-mindedness is an important attribute of the successful rider. There are many aspects of riding that will deter the faint-hearted. A fall, a bite, a kick or some other misfortune may deter any but the most determined. This determination must be tempered with patience and understanding and a very high degree of self-control. Whilst the rider or horseman must be firm and resolute, loss of temper or brutal treatment of the horse only ever results in the human losing the battle and the horse getting the upper hand. The horse has a very good memory and he will sooner or later learn how to score over a trainer who does not have complete control over his own emotions.

The ability to remain firm and unruffled in the face of adversity is an important rider quality. No amount of arm waving, shouting or excitable behaviour on the part of the rider or groom will achieve a lasting result. That does not mean, however, that two or three good hard slaps with the whip at exactly the right moment, delivered to the hind-quarters without anger or revenge, will not create a lasting memory in the horse and discourage him from repeating the behaviour that warranted a reprimand.

The good horseman must be able to move confidently but safely around the horse. A pat on the neck, as a sign of approval or to let him know that you are there, will help to develop a relationship between the man and the horse as will speaking to him in a reassuring way. Baby talk and kissing and cuddling the horse play no part in proper horsemanship.

Patience and the ability to understand the difficulties that the horse encounters in his training must be developed in the rider. It will be seen in ensuing chapters that the rider's physical fitness is important and that repetition plays a positive role in training. It is well known that patience and tolerance tend to wane as one tires physically and mentally. In these circumstances the quality of training may deteriorate. Even when the horse is at his worst and appears to be determined not to understand or co-operate, the slightest sign of improvement must be rewarded. It is easy to understand the difficulty the rider may have in doing this, particularly when he is tired and feeling that to slap the horse with the whip would do him, the rider, more good. It is the well-being of the horse that must be considered first.

There is sometimes a tendency amongst riders to be too greedy. Knowing when to finish a training session is a skill that should be developed. On the morning when the horse first jumps a fence of 92cm (3ft) there is a temptation to put it up to 1m (3ft 3in). If he jumps that well, the temptation is to put it up to 1.06m (3ft 6in), at which he refuses. The question then arises: 'What is to be done next?' The answer is of course that the horse should have been rewarded when he jumped 92cm (3ft) for the first time and taken out for a hack in the woods or put on to some other training.

'Equestrian tact' is a well-used expression in the horse world. It means the ability to work in harmony with the horse, moulding his great strength and ability by the use of superior human intelligence, tact and knowledge of equine behaviour, to produce a relaxed co-operative horse.

The earliest written works on riding show that equestrianism has always been associated with gentlemanly behaviour. Good manners are expected of those who ride horses, not just because they improve the quality of life, but because the dangers inherent in horse riding are compounded if those involved do not conduct their activities with consideration for others. Riding is one of the few remaining sports in which good manners are not just desirable but compulsory.

Position, Manner and Attitude of the Rider

There are a number of sports in which it is very difficult, if not impossible, to make progress unless a correct, basic technique has been established. Golf, skiing and swimming are obvious examples. There are instances in which competitors in these sports reach international standard whilst defying all the fundamental rules but these are the exceptions rather than the rule.

Academic works on how the horse should be ridden have been produced for the past two thousand years and more. They reflect contemporary thought and in some cases revolutionary innovation on the art. The fundamentals of riding that are taught today are the result of many years of study and are not the personal whim of one trainer or authority. Whilst there are slight differences in detail between the various national schools, the general aims of European riding are almost identical. Outside Europe in the Orient and America, in the more esoteric equestrian world, the aims are, at times, rather different.

The aim of the European style of riding is threefold:

1 To give the horse a well-balanced load to carry. A well-balanced load is easier to carry than an unbalanced load.
2 To enable the rider to apply the aids with the legs, the seat and the hands quickly and effectively.
3 To give an elegant appearance. Riding is a combination of sport and art and as such must be pleasing to the eye.

The position of the rider in the saddle will vary to a degree depending on the type of riding he is engaged in. The flat-race jockey rides with a very short stirrup and in a crouched position to enable the horse to gallop at full speed. He only has to maintain this position for a few minutes at most. The show jumper rides in a balanced, forward position to allow the horse full use of his back and to be able to go with him when jumping. In dressage the rider sits full in the bottom of the saddle with a long leg in a position in which he can create maximum impulsion and minute control. The general-purpose rider adopts some qualities from each of these techniques.

The seat
The true horseman will develop a fundamental seat that can be adjusted to suit all disciplines, as the expert three-day event rider will demonstrate.

Fig 5 The rider's position viewed from the side. She sits full in the bottom of the saddle; the body upright and the chin up

The first requirement of a good seat is that the rider should be able to sit in the lowest part of the saddle with equal weight on both seat-bones. In some schools of riding it is necessary to put more weight on one side of the seat at times to create a particular effect. This cannot possibly be achieved until the rider is capable of sitting with equal weight on both seat-bones. To achieve this it is necessary to be very supple in the hip joint, the large joint where the top of the femur fits into the pelvis. This joint is surrounded by massive muscles and any tension here will result in a loss of mobility of the joint. It is necessary to be able to sit full on the seat, not on the inside of the thigh or kneeling on the knees. Common faults are to sit forward on the fork or to tuck the coccyx underneath, rounding the back.

The body

The shape of the upper part of the body is important. The rider's body weight should be maintained directly over the seat. A straight vertical line should pass from the ear, through the shoulder, the point of the hip to the back of the

Figs 6 and 7 Two incorrect seats: Fig 6 shows the rider tipping forward and sitting on the fork, and in Fig 7 the rider is round in the back, leaning backwards and sitting on the coccyx. The lower leg is too far forward to apply the aids correctly

Figs 8 and 9 The rider's position, when viewed from both front and rear, is straight, symmetrical and well balanced

heel. The rider should carry his head in a natural position with his nose and his chin pointed directly between the horse's ears. The neck must come out from the shoulders and not where the knot of a tie would be. The rider must be able to look up or down, left or right as he wishes, but the important point is that the head should generally be held straight and not tilted up or down, left or right. The head is a large, influential part of the body as those who have studied gymnastics or dancing will know. Where the head goes the rest of the body tends to follow consequently it is very important that the rider should be in control of the position of his head.

The body must be held upright but without tension. The shoulders should be dropped back and down with the chest carried up and out. If the rider thinks of stretching the distance between the bottom rib to the hip bone, making the abdomen long and flat not short and round, the correct shape of the torso will be achieved without tension. When sitting correctly the hips should be forward, making a dip in the rider's back, about where the waist belt goes. A hollow back, however, must be avoided.

Straightness is an important aspect of the rider's position. If the horse is required to go straight then the rider must sit straight. The shoulders must be level, never one up and one down nor one forward and one back. A line drawn through the rider's shoulders from side to side should, for all practical purposes, be parallel to a line drawn through the horse's shoulders. This line should also be parallel to a line drawn through the rider's hips from side to side.

The legs
The position of the legs is important for two reasons:

1 They must be in the correct position for the rider to apply the leg aids correctly.
2 Incorrect carriage of the legs will affect the position of the upper part of the body. The lower leg carried too far forward tends to tip the upper body backwards. The lower leg carried too far back tends to tip the upper body forward.

The length of the stirrups depends upon the work being done and the position in which the rider wishes to sit. In the general-purpose seat the stirrup must be long enough to enable the rider to sit deep in the saddle when required. It must be short enough to enable the rider to take his weight directly off the horse's back, putting it on to his knees and the stirrup iron, when jumping or galloping. The dressage rider requires his leg to be longer, ensuring that he can sit fully in the bottom of the saddle, facilitating the use of his seat and back as an aid. He requires a good length of leg to enable him to have the control required in competition dressage. The dressage saddle is designed with a shorter, deeper seat, a long straight-cut flap and the stirrup bar set more under the seat to help the rider develop his position.

The ball of the foot should be on the stirrup iron and

the stirrup leather should hang vertically. This puts the leg in the best position to apply the leg aids correctly and helps with the position of the upper part of the body. The well-balanced rider never vacates this lower-leg position (except when applying the quarter-controlling or canter aids). This is demonstrated by the expert jumping rider who may at times be left behind or lose his balance when jumping. Balance is easily recovered if the lower leg remains correctly positioned. If it is swung violently back, pushed forward or taken away from the horse's side, balance can easily be lost in an emergency.

To ensure springiness in the hip, the knee and the ankle joints the heel should be carried a little lower than the toe. The feel with the foot on the stirrup iron should be soft and springy not dull and heavy. The joints of the rider's legs act like shock absorbers maintaining balance and agility. Stiff hips, knees and ankles result in poor balance, agility and co-ordination.

Effective leg aids are made from a still leg. The rider with the still leg encourages the horse to respond to the smallest leg aid, the rider with the leg that continuously moves encourages the horse to ignore the leg aid. Supple hip, knee and ankle joints help to keep the leg still enabling the body to move without affecting the leg. It helps if the sole of the boot is parallel to the ground with no twist in the ankle inwards or outwards. The foot should hang from the ankle in a natural way enabling as much of the inside of the leg as possible to be softly but surely wrapped around the horse's side without gripping. Gripping with the knee and the inside of the thigh tends to squeeze the rider up and out of the saddle. Grip, however, must be developed for use in emergencies. Sometimes when jumping a mistake is made, in polo one is ridden off hard or when schooling a young horse he shies or rears due to inexperience, the ability to grip is clearly necessary in this sort of circumstance. The part of the leg that is used for gripping is not the knee or the thigh but the dip in the leg between the bottom of the knee and the top of the calf muscle. This is much more secure than gripping with the knee and thigh, or even worse, the heels. In emergencies the heels are pushed down and out and a closer contact is taken with the leg just below the knee.

Effective riding is done mainly with the rider's legs. They are an essential element in balance and security and play a major role in creating impulsion and guiding the horse.

The hands

'The rider's hands belong to, and should be part of, the horse.' This remark may seem strange at first, to the uninitiated, but as knowledge and experience grow its significance will become clear. The hands must guide and control, but never restrict. They must be carried in such a way that the rider can keep a sure, steady even contact on the horse's mouth through the reins and the bit. They must not restrict the natural movement of the horse's head and neck which is so important in the establishment of his natural paces.

The hands should be carried in a workmanlike position, neither too high nor too low. The left hand is carried on the left-hand side of the horse's neck and the right hand on the right-hand side. The thumb and forefinger are on top with the knuckles to the outside. If the rider thinks about making a straight line from the elbow through the little finger to the bit in the horse's mouth he will carry his hands at about the correct height. This is a good guide for all work whether in collected, working, medium or extended paces, or, when galloping and jumping.

Good hands begin in a relaxed neck and shoulders. The shoulder and elbow joints must be soft and supple. The wrist is soft, the hand being a straight extension of the arm, with no curl in the wrist. The carriage of the hands and arms must not restrict the natural movement of the horse's head and neck. A soft, relaxed elbow and shoulder will allow the horse free, natural use of his head and neck whilst the rider maintains a sure rein contact.

The elbows should be dropped softly to the rider's side, neither clamped down tight so that the rider is hugging himself, nor lifted with the forearm up and out. The inside of the sleeve should brush softly on the side of the jacket.

Whilst the correct posture of the rider is a fundamental

element of good horsemanship, striving to achieve it must not detract from the rider's suppleness or effectiveness. He must be able to move with the horse, blending the movements of his body into those of the horse, so that both horse and rider work in harmony moving in unison together as one animal. In each of the basic paces there is a swing in the horse's back which the rider must be able to feel and follow with the swing of his body. Each beat of the pace and each individual footfall of the horse should be felt by the rider through his seat. This will only be achieved when the rider is correct, balanced and supple in his position on the horse.

Physical Fitness

The degree of physical fitness required by a truly effective rider is no less than that which is necessary in any other physically demanding sport. It is a sad sight, not infrequently seen, at the end of a point-to-point or the speed and endurance phase of a horse trial where the horse is hampered by the encumbrance of a rider who has run out of breath and is insufficiently fit to give the horse the help that he requires and deserves over the last fence.

Together with a strong heart/lung system the rider requires the suppleness, strength and agility of a gymnast, combined with the balance and co-ordination of a dancer. The competition rider must ride for a minimum of two hours a day if he is to stay riding fit. He will probably combine this with other suppling and stretching exercises and work to improve general fitness such as jogging.

Overweight riders, with very few exceptions, are suffering from a self-inflicted handicap. The extra unnecessary strain put upon a horse by an overweight rider is obvious, the other difficulties that it causes are loss of suppleness, co-ordination, agility and balance on the part of the rider, all of which are vital elements in effective horsemanship. It is extremely difficult to reduce body weight by exercising. The well-exercised body looks better because muscle-tone and general health are improved but the only way to control body weight is by careful control of the diet.

It is only fair and sensible for the rider to aim to be at

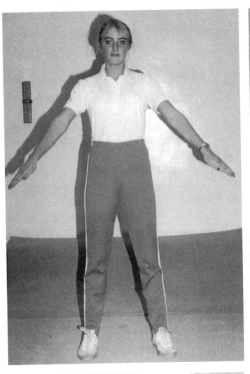

Figs 10-15 Fitness exercises for the rider

least as fit as his horse, if not fitter. There are times when the horse positively requires the agility, balance and strength of the rider to assist him in his task. It is not sufficient to be only a passive partner in the horse and rider relationship.

The Aids

The signals that the rider makes to the horse with his legs, seat and hands are known as aids. They are reinforced by the rider's voice, the whip and the spurs. The legs, seat, hands and voice are known as natural aids and the whip and spur as artificial aids.

There are, therefore, very few aids at the rider's disposal to ask the horse to perform a wide range of activities. The horse may be asked to walk, trot, canter, gallop, jump, turn, stop, move forwards and sideways at the same time and to perform many other physical exercises. To achieve all this the rider can only squeeze with one or other or both legs, push with his seat, or, feel either or both reins. Clearly it can be seen from this that a subtle blend of leg, seat and hand aids is required, used in many different ways, to train and ride the horse effectively.

In general terms the rider's legs and seat encourage the horse to go forward with energy. The hands, through the reins and the bit, receive, guide and control that energy.

Leg aids
In the early stages of training the horse and rider both legs are used, just behind the girth, to ask the horse to go forward. Quick squeezes with both calves should be effective. If they are not the leg aids should be applied again accompanied by a tap with the whip. The leg should not be drawn backwards and upwards but used directly inwards with the stirrup leather continuing to hang vertically. The principle of using the leg aid is *not* that the rider inflicts such pain on the horse that he goes forward so that the kicking stops. Once the leg aid has been obeyed it should be discontinued and the leg kept still. When he responds to the leg aids they should be reduced in strength until the minimum aid is used to obtain the required effect. Whilst, in general, kicking with the legs is counter-productive and causes horses to become 'dead to the leg' there are times, in an emergency, when the horse must be ridden strongly forward by using both legs together, very vigorously, eg when he is refusing at a jump or is hesitating unnecessarily at a hazard of some sort. It is then sometimes necessary to drive the horse forward with the legs, but it should be the exception rather than the rule. The legs are used in conjunction with the seat to create and maintain impulsion (see page 71).

The rider's legs are also used to keep the horse straight by controlling the hindquarters. If the hindquarters swing out on a corner, or on a circle, the rider's outside leg is drawn back to move the quarters in, so that the footprints made by the horse's hind feet follow in the same line of tracks made by the fore feet. In their quarter-controlling role, the rider's legs also ask the horse to make his lateral work, or work on two tracks, by moving the hindquarters sideways.

Fig 16 The correctly fitted spur; it should be high on the boot and parallel to the ground. Fig 17 This spur is incorrectly fitted

In both upward and downward transitions both legs are used together to ask the horse to walk or trot. When he is asked to canter the rider's outside leg is drawn back to give the command. These aids are discussed in detail on pages 46–7.

Spurs
When the horse is fully obedient to the leg aid, spurs can be used to refine these aids. In correct horsemanship they are only used when the horse is required to produce greater impulsion and collection and are usually used in conjunction with the double bridle. They are never used on young horses and should only be worn by competent riders on trained horses. Only blunt spurs are worn, their length is unimportant provided that they are correctly used. The expert rider, wearing spurs, will still be able to apply the leg aids where necessary, without the spur coming into effect.

Unfortunately spurs are, in some cases, part of correct dress, in hunting clothes or military uniform for example.

They are *not* intended to make reluctant or lazy horses go faster.

Whip
The schooling whip is an important part of correct riding and training. It should be about 1m (3ft) in length and not so thin that it is sharp. The short, or jumping whip is useful when competing in jumping competitions or riding across country. Its use in schooling is, however, limited. The long schooling whip is carried to enable the rider to reinforce the leg aid without spoiling the hand. It is carried so that it hangs just behind the rider's leg, and can be used with sharp taps close to where the leg aid is applied. It should be used in conjunction with the leg to encourage the horse to respond to the leg aid. Due to its cutting nature, this whip should never be used to punish the horse. It is usually carried in the rider's inside hand as it is most often the inside leg that requires reinforcement. However, this is relatively unimportant, and the rider need be in no hurry to change the whip from one hand to the other when he changes the rein.

When the short whip is used both reins must be taken in one hand and the whip turned so that it comes out of the hand between the thumb and forefinger. It is then used behind the rider's leg on the flank or hindquarters. On occasions, the whip is used to reprimand the horse, perhaps when he kicks, refuses to go forward or is deliberately disobedient. In these circumstances two or three slaps with the whip should be applied to accompany the act that warranted them. The 'association of ideas' is important here: it is no use reprimanding the horse minutes after he has misbehaved. The offending act and the slap with the whip should be as close together as possible.

The seat
The aids made with the seat are important in making the horse go forward and in creating impulsion. These aids are variously described as seat aids, weight aids or back aids. The fact is that all three of these elements are used in combination as the seat is really the rider's body weight.

It is applied through the seat by the use of the muscles in the rider's back. It can only be used correctly and effectively when the rider has established a well-balanced, deep, independent seat. However this aid is used, its effect is to send the horse forward, but, when used incorrectly on a horse that is hollow in the back and above the bit, whilst it sends him forward with greater vigour, it almost certainly makes him more hollow and increases the resistance. No amount of driving with the seat will encourage the hollow horse to bring his hind legs underneath him. It follows, therefore, that the seat aid can only be really effective when the horse accepts the bit and the weight of the rider on his back, without resistance.

Once the horse is accepting the bit, is rounded in his outline, with a certain amount of engagement of the hind legs, then the seat aids are vital in creating impulsion and influencing the horse. Before this stage, excessive use of the seat as a driving aid is usually counter-productive. This does not mean that the rider should not sit fully on his seat when applicable, in all his work, but it does mean that he must be able to leave his body weight fully on the seat, in a passive way, without it influencing the horse or driving him forward.

The use of the seat as an aid requires the rider to be soft in the waist and supple in the hips. This enables him to use his body weight in rhythm with the swing of the horse's back encouraging greater activity without unbalancing or interrupting the pace. It is an essential part of correct equitation that the rider should be able to blend the movement of his body into the swing of the horse's back, at all paces, without making more movement than the horse is naturally making for himself. Only then will he be able to influence the horse by the use of his body weight. The ability of the rider to sit in the bottom of the saddle, fully on his seat, the hips straight to the front, and with equal weight on each seat-bone is a fundamental requirement in the use of the seat aids.

The hands

The hands receive, guide and control the energy created by the legs and the seat. Until that energy has been created, the

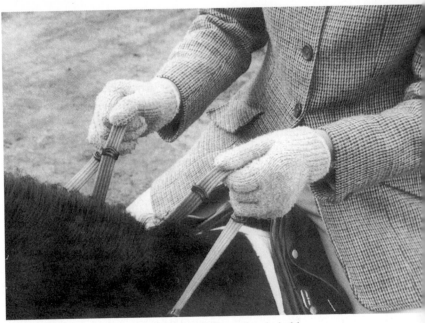

Fig 18 The reins of the snaffle bridle, correctly held
Fig 19 The reins of the double bridle, correctly held

hands cannot be correctly used. Hence the widely accepted maxim that 'the legs are always used before the hands'. When the horse is becoming established in his training, it is the fingers that apply the aids and not the hands. In the early stages it is necessary to use the opening rein to invite the horse to bend his neck to the left or right, encouraging him to look where he is going, and hence training him to change direction. When using the hands as part of the aids to turn a horse, they should not be used like the handlebars of a bicycle or the steering wheel in a motor car, since the horse is capable of going straight forward with his neck bent hard to the left or right. They should, instead, be used to send a polite request down the rein to the bit, which should result in the horse responding by making a willing turn.

Good hands are those that allow the horse to go energetically and freely forward, whilst keeping a sure, steady contact on the bars of his mouth, through the reins and the bit. To understand this fully, the rider must appreciate the effect that the bit has on the horse. First, the bit lies on the bars of the mouth. The bars are the part of the jaw between the corner, incisor teeth and the first of the premolar teeth on the lower jaw. When the rein is taken up, the bit wrinkles the corners of the lips and closes around the tongue. If the bit is too wide and a tight noseband is fitted there is a possibility that the joint of the bit will touch the roof of the horse's mouth particularly if he has a low, soft palate. If the reins are roughly used, it is likely that the bit will come into contact with the molar teeth. If a dropped noseband is fitted, pressure is put on the front of the nose. The bit, through the bridle, applies pressure to the poll. The bit that incorporates a curb chain brings pressure to bear on the chin groove. It is obvious therefore that a great deal of discomfort, if not pain, can be inflicted by the rider's hands. The horse is more likely to accept a sure steady contact on his mouth, than an unsteady varying contact. The object of all trainers is to ride with a light rein, but a light rein, with a constantly varying contact is less acceptable to the horse than a slightly stronger and steadier contact that allows freedom of movement.

Eventually the rein aids must be made by squeezing

with the fingers rather as though holding a rubber ball in the hand and squeezing it. The aid cannot possibly be made in this way through loose or floppy reins. The onus for maintaining the rein contact is entirely with the rider hence the importance of the correct manner of holding the reins in the fingers and of soft, supple elbows and shoulders which allow the horse to adjust the height of his head and the length of his neck as he wishes, without varying the contact of the bit on his mouth.

The length of the reins play a part in the use of the rein aids. Whilst it is, to a degree, a matter of personal preference the reins should not be so short that there is no bend in the elbow. This detracts from the ability to allow the horse to vary the height of his head and the length of his neck. They should not be so long that the elbows come behind the back as this also detracts from the rider's ability to maintain a sure but 'allowing' contact.

The hand on the inside of the bend of the horse, asks for the bend by short, intermittent squeezes with the fingers. The hand on the outside of the bend receives and controls the energy created by the legs. It also controls the bend in the horse's neck.

The principle of any aid application is that once a response has been made to a rein aid, it should be discontinued and the hands kept still. Still hands are those which remain still whilst allowing the horse freedom to go forward. Only from these can correct aids be applied. The feel of the reins in the hands is important too. Reins that are too thin are difficult to feel as are those that are too thick. Once again it is a matter of personal preference, but whilst continental, plaited or rubber reins are very good for racing, cross-country riding and jumping, a soft, leather rein of a thickness to suit the hand is best for schooling. A riding trainer can tell a student what he should physically do with his hands, but only study, experience and the use of the imagination will result in the establishment of good hands.

Voice
The voice is an aid which can be used to good effect. It is unlikely that the horse will ever understand a wide

human vocabulary, as the dog will, but his memory is good, and he will certainly respond to the voice. The number of words that he is required to learn should be kept short: 'walk', 'walk on', 'trot', 'canter', and 'woah' are probably sufficient. It is the *tone* of the voice, and not the individual word, that will achieve the required result. A long, relaxing, drawn-out word will encourage the horse to slow down or make a downward transition. A sharp, executive word of command will encourage him to jump along with greater activity. 'Clicking' the tongue is a voice aid used by many trainers and riders to good effect. It usually makes the horse increase his activity when asked to do so when approaching a fence to jump, or even when being loaded into a trailer. Horses are also capable of learning verbal instructions in the stable. If the word 'foot' is used each time the groom lifts up a foot to pick it out, the horse learns to lift his foot when he hears that word. When mucking out, if the word 'over' is used each time he is asked to move to the other side of the box, he will soon learn to move on that verbal command. It is often an advantage, when either mounted or dismounted, to 'growl' at the horse when he misbehaves, or when he is being admonished with the whip. He learns that this tone of voice is a sign of the rider's or trainer's disapproval. He will also respond to an encouraging word, used together with a pat on the neck as a sign of approval.

The overall principle of applying the aids is that '. . . maximum response is required from the horse, from minimum effort on the part of the rider'. To this end, whilst the aids should be quiet and inconspicuous, they must be effective. There are some differences of opinion on the application of the aids between the major riding schools of the world, but in general, they have a common aim. The aids that have been detailed are those of the Spanish Riding School of Vienna on which British riding is founded. It is recommended that the student of equitation should establish one school of thought clearly in his mind before he considers the principles of several. A clear understanding of one school will make the understanding of the others much easier.

Basic Movements

There are fundamental aids to ask the horse to perform the transitions and basic school movements which make him a useful riding horse.

To walk from halt

The reins are taken up to a working length and both legs are closed against the horse's sides to get his attention, but without moving forward. Once the horse is attentive, the rider is sitting correctly and the reins are the correct length, the rider closes both legs directly inwards with quick squeezes just behind the girth. At the same time he softens the feel in the hand allowing the horse to walk forward. Once he is walking forward the leg aids are discontinued.

Continual kicking with both or alternate legs to keep the horse walking with energy only serves to make the horse dead to the leg and eventually to ignore the leg aids altogether. Should more energy be required, the leg aid must be correctly applied, if necessary accompanied by the whip. There is more, however, to getting the horse to go forward than continual use of the leg aids. If the rider allows the horse to nod his head and neck, in rhythm with his stride, by being soft and supple in the elbow and shoulder, and allows the swing in the horse's back by being soft in the waist and supple in the hips, allowing the swing of his body, to blend, softly, into the swing of the horse's back, he will, without excessive use of the legs, encourage the horse to walk out.

To trot from walk or halt

The reins are shortened to a length that will allow the contact to be maintained through the transition and in the first steps in trot. The horse's attention is obtained with a half-halt (see page 78) and both legs are applied, with quick squeezes, just behind the girth. The feel in the hand is softened to allow the horse to trot.

To canter from trot or walk

If this transition is made from trot, it is best from sitting trot, in a corner or on a circle. In preparation to canter the rider must first ensure that the horse is going forward with sufficient impulsion, if he is not, the leg aids are applied just behind the girth. It must then be confirmed that the horse is bent a little in the direction in which he is going. If he is not, a feel with the fingers of the inside hand, whilst keeping the contact with the outside rein, together with a feel with the inside leg, should achieve this.

With the impulsion and bend correct, the rider is ready to ask for canter. As he approaches the corner, or the point at which he has decided to canter, he brings back his outside leg – well behind the girth – to give one clear canter aid. He gives the executive word of command 'canter now' with his outside leg, as it is the horse's outside hind leg that starts the canter stride. The importance of this early training will be seen, when it comes to making flying changes later in his work.

Downward transitions

The downward transitions are: canter to trot; trot to walk; walk to halt; trot to halt; canter to walk and canter to halt. The aids to make these transitions are, for all practical purposes, the same. It is a matter of the degree to which they are given that achieves the result.

Downward transitions are generally more difficult to make well than upward transitions. This is due to the young or untrained horse being out of balance, carrying too much weight on the forehand, and having insufficient engagement of the hind legs. Half-halts should therefore be made before the transition in an attempt to improve the horse's balance. To do this the rider drops his seat softly down into the saddle and closes both legs, just behind the girth. This encourages the horse to bring his hind legs underneath him. It is followed by intermittent squeezing with the fingers of the outside hand until the desired result has been achieved.

Turning left, turning right, circling left and circling right

Once again, the aids that are made to perform these movements are very similar. It is the degree to which they are applied that achieves the result. The horse is unable to make a right-angled turn but he can make an accurate circle or part of a circle. The turn to the left or right should be thought of as a quarter of a circle. These turns or circles must be large in diameter at first, perhaps not less than 20m (22yd), becoming smaller as training progresses. Again, the horse is prepared to turn or circle with the half-halt to gain his attention and improve his balance. He is invited to turn or circle to the left or the right by feeling the inside rein. The contact is maintained with the outside rein to ensure that the neck does not bend excessively. The inside leg, just behind the girth, maintains the impulsion, whilst the outside leg is ready to be used in its quarter-controlling role, to prevent the hindquarters from swinging out, should they tend to do so.

These are the basic aids for riding the horse. In Chapter 4 the development of these aids to achieve the various suppling exercises and more advanced school movements will be discussed.

When studying the aids used to convey our requirements to the horse, there are a number of criteria which should be considered:

1 In the first stages of training the horse and rider both legs are used to ask the horse to go forward. Early in the training the rider should be encouraged to understand that the horse must go forward from the inside leg aid and that the outside leg is the quarter-controlling leg. The importance of this will be realised when it comes to lateral work.
2 To ensure that the aids can be made with maximum effect, all transitions are made with the body upright.
3 The horse cannot be compelled to comply with the aids, no matter how vigorously they are applied. Only with his willing co-operation will they be successful. The rider must use his superior intelligence to persuade the horse to comply with his wishes. Physical force only creates resistance in the horse and whilst some short-term results may be achieved, no lasting good is ever done by its use.

3 Training the Young Horse

Correct, progressive basic training is essential from birth no matter which equestrian discipline the horse is to be used for. It must be firm but compassionate teaching by repetition and reward with admonition when required.

The horse has a good memory but little reasoning power. He responds well to routine, repetitive training with variety, and the principle of the association of ideas.

At the earliest possible stage, certainly within the first few hours of life, the foal must be introduced to the human being. He must be stroked and handled in the first twenty-four hours and a foal slip fitted in the first forty-eight hours. Weather permitting, the mare that has foaled in the stable will be turned out to grass within the first forty-eight hours of the foal's life. This gives the handler the opportunity to lead the foal behind his mother, holding the foal slip, but with an arm around the quarters to urge him forward from behind, rather than pulling from in front. A coloured show-jumping pole, put on the ground across the gateway into the field, will ensure that the foal steps over the pole behind his mother each time that he goes out or comes in. This very elementary introduction to 'jumping' may well make training very much easier in four years' time.

This firm but tactful handling of the foal will help to ensure successful backing at a later stage. The foal must be made thoroughly confident in human company: his feet must be picked up and handled; he can be brushed lightly; his tail and ears can be touched and his mouth inspected. Whilst the foal must be trained to be friendly and come up to meet you in the field he must not be allowed to become playful or over-familiar. The dividing line between being friendly and disrespectful must be clearly established by the trainer, if necessary with a harsh word or a slap. Titbits should be prohibited as they frequently teach the horse to nip or be aggressive if they come to be expected.

Above all the foal must be taught to lead correctly from both sides. This is so much easier to do when young than to leave him unled until he is two- or three- years old and strong enough to make this part of his training very difficult.

Apart from the preparation for backing, this early training will prepare him for the many other aspects of daily life that he will encounter. Shoeing, worming, teeth rasping, veterinary treatment, wearing rugs and bandages. Travelling in a trailer or horse box will all be easier if introduced to the foal and not left until he is a mature horse.

After this initial training the young horse is usually turned away to grass until his serious work is started towards the end of his third year. The object of this period is to allow him to grow and mature sufficiently to be backed. He should not, however, be left entirely untouched. Whilst he will not be ready to start work until he is about three and a half, it is essential that he is handled daily. His feet must be picked out, he must be lightly groomed, mane and tail kept in good order, and if possible he should be travelled to a horse show from time to time and perhaps shown in hand. All this will make backing the horse very much easier. If he is introduced to the horse show as a youngster he will hear the loud speaker, hear the band playing and generally experience the excitement created at a show. It is far better to introduce him to all this as a yearling or a two-year-old, than to take him to his first show as a ridden four-year-old.

At three-and-a-half to four years of age, depending on the way that he has matured, the young horse will be ready to start serious training.

Lungeing

Assuming that he has been led in hand successfully from both sides in walk and trot and will respond to the voice aids, has worn a rug, and is generally well handled, the next stage is to start to teach him to lunge. Here the trainer works on the horse on a lunge rein, in a circle with the trainer standing in the centre.

The advantages of lungeing are:

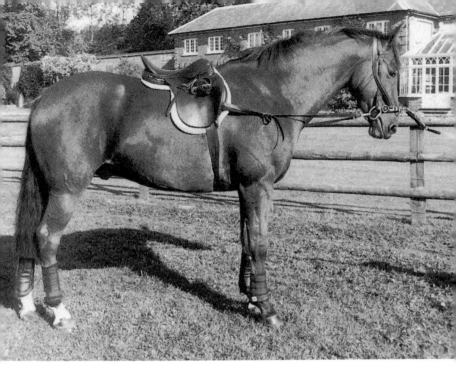

Fig 20 Correctly dressed for lungeing

1 It is good physical training for the horse, building muscle and improving suppleness, co-ordination, agility and balance.
2 It helps to establish the basic paces with good rhythm, tempo and cadence, without the encumbrance of the rider on the horse's back.
3 It teaches the horse to obey the voice aids.
4 It gives the opportunity to fit the bridle, bit and saddle to the horse before he is ridden.
5 It continues the general handling of the horse, increasing the chances of establishing willing submission.

Selection of the area in which the horse is to be lunged is important. An indoor school is ideal but not always available. An outside schooling area with a sound fence is good, but in the absence of either of these a small sheltered paddock should be selected, away from too many distractions. When lungeing in a paddock, it is best to choose a corner which provides fencing on two adjacent sides: this usually helps in the early stages whilst the circle is being established. Whatever location is used, the going should be good, so that there is no chance of the young horse slipping with all the attendant problems that may cause.

To be able to lunge with any confidence, the following equipment is required:

1 A lungeing cavesson of a suitable size for the horse. A good fit is particularly important as control may be lost if the lungeing cavesson is too big and damage may be caused if it is too small.
2 A lunge rein, about 6.5m (22ft) in length with a strong spring hook on one end, attached to a swivel, with a loop of about 20cm (8in) on the other. It can be made of nylon or strong webbing, the latter tends to be softer on the hands.
3 A lungeing roller with a breast girth, rings to attach side reins and two other strong 'D' rings for long-reining.
4 Boots or bandages for all four legs together with over-reach boots for the forefeet.
5 Side reins.
6 A lungeing whip.

At first it will be an advantage to have an assistant to lead the horse on the circle. He will walk on the side nearest to the trainer, leading the horse by a short rein attached to the centre ring on the lungeing cavesson. This method is better than the assistant holding the lunge rein or the bridle. The task of the assistant is to ensure that the horse responds to the trainer's voice. When the horse is told to 'walk on' by the trainer the assistant must lead him forward, patting him on the neck if he responds well. If he does not respond to the command, the assistant must lead the horse forward as the trainer encourages him with the lungeing whip. It is essential that the horse walks willingly forward with the assistant at his shoulder. Under no circumstances must he be allowed to hang back being dragged forward by the assistant.

As the command 'whoa' is given by the trainer, the

assistant should feel the rein, asking the horse to halt. A good response should be rewarded by a pat on the neck and a congratulatory word.

When the words of command are understood and the horse is responding well, the assistant can move away along the lunge rein towards the trainer, and eventually leave the circle. It may be necessary for the assistant to return to his task if the work regresses and the words of command are being ignored.

It is sometimes argued that the assistant should walk on the outside so that he is not between the trainer and the horse. This is possible but it entails the assistant walking quite fast and may create a tendency for the horse to bend his neck to the outside which is undesirable. There is also the possibility that the assistant may be kicked as he moves away should the horse react upon finding himself free on the other end of the lunge rein.

Once the horse will walk and halt on the lunge, he can be asked to trot. It may or may not be necessary to have an assistant here, but if in doubt, it is better to err on the side of caution. As the horse's balance, suppleness and obedience improve, he can be asked to canter. He will need the largest circle possible, commensurate with the trainer being able to keep control. All the work should be done equally on both reins and care should be taken to see that the animal is not worked for too long. Lungeing is physically demanding and may put considerable strain on the joints of the young horse, particularly the hocks. Aside from the physical aspect, the risk of boredom should be considered.

The size of the lungeing circle is important for the young horse. As a rough guide, for a horse of 16 hands, the circle should not be less than about 16m (17^1/$_2$yd) in diameter. A larger horse will require a larger circle and a smaller horse may be able to work on a smaller circle. It is clearly dangerous to lunge on too small a circle, but it must not be so big that the horse cannot be reached with the whip, or cause the trainer to lose control. Experience will find the size of circle on which the horse works best.

The words of command should be clear and encouraging. It is best to use a cautionary word of command, perhaps a drawn out 'and', and an executive word of command 'ter-rot'. In the upward transitions the cautionary word of command should be drawn out and the executive word of command sharp. For example, 'aaaand ter-rot'. The words of command for a downward transition should all be drawn out, for example, 'aaaand waaaalk'. The actual words used are unimportant as the tone of the voice will achieve the desired result. However, if universal words of command can be agreed upon, it will make the passing of a horse from one trainer to another easier.

The lungeing whip is used for two purposes. Aimed out towards the hocks and used in conjunction with the appropriate words of command, it encourages the horse to go forward. Used towards the shoulder, it encourages him to stay out on the circle should he tend to fall in towards the trainer. Having touched the horse with the whip it is then, usually, only necessary to point it towards his hocks to encourage him forward. If necessary, it should be flicked at his hocks. Cracking the whip must be avoided as the sound makes the horse jump. He must learn to accept a crack or a bang without jumping forward from it. If the lash of the whip is allowed to trail out behind the trainer it is easy to flick it towards the horse with accuracy. If it lies in a bunch on the ground in front of the trainer, it is difficult to do anything with it.

Whilst lungeing, the trainer should stand in a relaxed, balanced way, ready to move in any direction. To start with, it may be necessary for him to walk in a circle, a little behind the horse, to ensure that the horse goes forward. Eventually when the horse lunges well, the trainer should stand still in the middle of the circle, pivoting around his left foot as he lunges to the left, and around his right foot as he lunges to the right. This will help to establish the accuracy of the circle. He must, however, be ready to move in any direction should the need arise. Any tendency to wander about whilst lungeing should be avoided.

The rein is usually held in tidy loops in the left hand when working to the left and in the right hand when working to the right. This leaves the other hand free to use the whip. Sometimes the rein is held in one hand and

Fig 21 A practical way to hold the lunge rein

the spare loops and the whip in the other. Provided that the selected method is safe and effective, it makes little difference. Twists in the rein should be avoided as these tend to spoil the feel in the hand. If the rein passes between the third finger and the little finger to the centre ring of the lungeing cavesson (see Fig 21) the feel in the hand with the lunge rein can be similar to the feel that one aims for with the bridle rein. The spare end of the rein should be wound in tidy loops ready to be dropped to lengthen the rein, or gathered up to shorten it. The trainer's elbow and shoulder joints should be soft and supple to allow some give and take in the contact of the rein. He should aim to keep the rein straight with a steady contact, allowing it to be slack or to fall into loops can be dangerous.

The lungeing cavesson should be a snug fit. If it is too loose it may rub and the outside cheek piece may pull forward into the horse's eye. The noseband should be tight enough to prevent slipping and the throat lash a snug fit to keep the cheek pieces in place. A variation of the lunge cavesson is the Wels cavesson. Here the noseband is fitted below the bit rather as the dropped noseband is fitted. This is very severe and should be handled with care, but it is particularly useful for lungeing spoilt or difficult horses.

Fig 22 A properly fitted lungeing cavesson

Fig 23 A correctly fitted snaffle bridle

Boots or bandages, with over-reach boots on the forefeet, are fitted to the horse when lungeing. This simple precaution is taken to protect the legs in circumstances where he might be fresh and playful, or his co-ordination is not fully established, causing him to strike into, or kick himself.

Young or untrained horses can be quite strong on the

lunge and as a safety precaution it is advisable for the trainer to wear gloves. In fact, in any dismounted work, where leading horses is involved, gloves are an essential piece of equipment.

Bitting

Once the young horse is lungeing obediently on both reins, the bit can be introduced to his mouth. A mild snaffle is preferred, fairly thick but not too heavy. It is essential

Fig 24 A properly fitted double bridle

that it is the correct width for the horse's mouth. If it is too narrow it pinches the lips and the jaw, if too wide the 'nut cracker' action is severe, and the joint in the bit may touch the roof of the mouth. A Fulmer cheek snaffle is recommended as it is easily kept in the correct position. The use of a mouthing bit is out-dated and not recommended. The aim is not to encourage the horse to 'champ' or play with the bit, but to encourage him to accept it lying softly on the bars of the mouth. The use of the mouthing bit, or leaving him tied up in the stable with the bit in his mouth, only encourages fidgeting and should be discouraged. If possible, a bit and the cheek pieces only should be fitted over the lungeing cavesson. Where this is not possible, a normal snaffle bridle can be used with the noseband and browband removed.

When the horse is lungeing quietly with the bit in his mouth, usually in quite a short time depending on how the permanent teeth have erupted and the tushes have grown, he can be introduced to the roller. If he has worn a rug this is unlikely to cause problems. It should be fitted quite loosely at first and a breast girth should be fitted before the roller buckles are done up. It is a serious setback if the roller is allowed to slip back round the horse's loins. A tail bandage tied from one side to the other, round his breast, is quite adequate for this purpose.

The lungeing work should be continued with the horse fitted with the bit and roller: walk, trot and canter with progressive transitions between the paces can be used. Once he is accepting the bit and the roller, side reins can be introduced. The object of side reins is twofold. Firstly, they help to keep the horse straight by discouraging him from bending his neck too much to the left or right. Secondly, they put a contact on to the bit which encourages the horse to seek for and accept a contact on the bars of his mouth. At first they should be fairly loose so that just the weight of the rein is resting on the bit. They must give sufficient freedom for the horse to adjust the height of his head and the length of his neck as he wishes. They must on no account pull his head down or in. The side reins must be of equal length, to shorten one or other only bends the

Fig 25 Jumping training on the lunge

neck and may result in loss of control of the shoulder on the opposite side to the bend. Plain leather side reins are quite satisfactory, those with rubber or elastic inserts may cause unnecessary problems which are best avoided. The side reins are fitted to the 'D' rings on the roller and to the rings of the snaffle bit. They should only be attached when they are to be used, connected when work on the lunge starts and disconnected as soon as it is finished. It is best not to use them at the walk in case they discourage the natural swing of the head and neck which is such an important feature of this pace.

Introducing the Saddle

After a few sessions in the roller and provided that there have been no serious setbacks, it can be replaced by a saddle. The stirrup irons should be run up the leathers and secured. A breast girth must be fitted to ensure that the saddle does not slip back. Provided that the young horse has been well handled from the start, it is usually not long before he will lunge quietly on both reins, respond to the trainer's voice to make the transitions and accept the bit and the saddle. The time that this will take varies between horses, but without hurrying any of the work, it can be achieved in two weeks or so.

The next stage in training is to lunge him over a pole on the ground. If a coloured pole was put across the gateway into his field when he was a foal this should present no difficulties. The number of poles can be increased to three at about 1.2–1.4m (4–4ft 6in) apart. This work is best done at the trot. He must approach the poles quietly and trot over them without a change in speed or tempo. In any lunge work over poles or jumps, boots or bandages should continue to be fitted and the side reins and saddle or roller removed.

When this is established, a jump can be introduced into the lunge work. Low cross-poles are suitable to start with, and a pole should be set against the inside wing stand to ensure that the lunge rein does not become tangled (see Fig 25). To ensure equal muscle development and suppleness the work over poles and jumps should be made equally on both reins.

Long-reining

Lungeing does not enable the trainer to teach the horse to respond to the rein aids. These include the aids to make transitions, (particularly downward transitions) and to turn left and right. The logical sequence is, therefore, to drive the horse in long reins. Two reins are required about 6.5–7.25m (22–24ft) long; lunge reins are quite suitable. They are fitted, at first, to the outside rings on the lungeing cavesson and later to the rings on the snaffle bit. In the British style of long-reining, they then pass through the 'D's on the roller, or through the stirrup irons which are secured by a cord under the horse as they were when the saddle was first fitted.

When the horse is being driven on a circle, the outside rein comes round behind him just above the hocks, to the trainer's hand, the inside rein passes through the inside stirrup iron to the trainer's hand. The height of the stirrup should be adjusted so that the reins remain about parallel to the ground. With the reins fitted in this way the trainer can work the horse in walk and trot on the circle and at walk by walking directly behind. The rein aids can then be used in conjunction with the voice to make transitions and to turn to the left and right. As the work advances, serpentines can be made and the direction of the circle changed by taking up the outside rein and letting the inside rein out, to allow him to turn. When driving on the circle the outside rein must be, if anything, rather loose to allow the horse to go forward. The trainer must understand that he is in a very strong position when he has the horse in long reins and the aids he gives can be severe. If the trainer is not very tactful and careful, he may easily make the horse over-bend. Carefully used, long-reining is a very good way to introduce the horse to working in public, on the road, in traffic, by farm machinery, or any other situation that may alarm him.

Backing

It is not possible to lay down a clear timetable for this programme of work largely due to the fact that no two horses are the same. Some take to being handled, lunged and backed very much more readily than others. It depends on their personality, temperament, the way in which they were originally handled, their breed, and the skill of the trainer. It is not unreasonable to expect the well-handled young horse to be ready to be backed by a lightweight rider, after about four to six weeks of leading in hand, lungeing and long-reining. There are systems of breaking young horses used in Australia, New Zealand and the United States where the animal is caught and tied up so that he cannot escape. With no other preparation the saddle and bridle are forcibly fitted and he is mounted by the rider. The young animal is probably too exhausted and unfit to protest greatly and after a time is ridden away. This is all done in an hour or less and it is claimed that the horse is broken. There is no doubt that the aim is achieved by very skilled trainers but the mental anguish and physical distress that the animal is put through are unacceptable. Without steady physical preparation, over a period of time, the horse cannot possibly be fit or strong enough to carry a saddle and a rider.

It therefore follows that no attempt should be made to back the young horse until he has developed confidence in his trainer and has been given the opportunity to build up his strength, co-ordination and balance over a period of careful training.

In many cases the trainer will back the horse by himself, without an assistant. This is often done as a matter of necessity as no assistant is available. There is no doubt, however, that backing the horse is a task best done by two people. When he is about to be backed for the first time the trainer will work him in hand on the lunge rein or driving reins in the usual way. The training session will end by the trainer disconnecting the side reins and holding the horse by the lunge rein, which is attached to the cavesson. A lightweight assistant stands first on the near side and then the off side holding the saddle by the pommel and the cantle, gently moving it about. A few slaps on the seat of the saddle and the flaps made with the palm of the hand will give the horse the feel of the saddle being used. The assistant will then, holding the pommel and the cantle again, make small jumps on both sides of the horse as though he is about to vault into the saddle. If this work is successful, the trainer will then give the rider a leg up, so that he can lean across the saddle and pat the horse on the opposite shoulder. When this has been done, the horse should be rewarded with a pat and an encouraging word and be put away. If the preceding work has been thoroughly carried out no difficulties should be encountered. No more than this should be attempted on the first day and it should be repeated over the next three or four days.

The understanding and knowledgable trainer will know when he can ask the horse to walk forward a few steps, whilst the rider lies across the saddle, talking to the horse and patting him on the opposite shoulder. Only five or six steps should be attempted at first. When this is successfully done the rider can put a leg over the saddle, keeping the top part of his body low over the horse's neck. All the time that this is being done the trainer and the rider should pat the horse and talk to him in an encouraging way. When this has been completed, the trainer can lead the horse forward in walk and after a while the rider can slowly take his body into the upright position. Whether or not stirrups are fitted to the saddle whilst the horse is first being backed is a matter of choice for the rider, some prefer to use stirrups and some are happier without them.

The trainer should lead the horse from the left and right, gradually passing over the verbal instructions to the rider, who begins to accompany the voice aids with leg and hand aids. As he gives the word of command 'walk on', he squeezes with both legs, slightly behind the girth. If the horse responds he is given a pat on the neck. As he gives the word of command 'whoa', he closes the legs softly and feels the outside rein. The same system is applied as the horse is asked to trot, still led by the trainer. This work is continued until the horse is confident and obedient whilst being led and carrying the rider.

The next stage is for the trainer to let the lunge rein out until the horse is working on a circle and now almost entirely under the command of the rider. When he does all the work willingly on the lunge, whilst carrying the rider, the rein can be disconnected and he can be ridden free in an enclosed space. As his experience grows he will be hacked out in the company of an experienced horse to continue his education and introduction to the outside world.

It is a mistake to rush this basic training and it is often to the trainer's advantage to go back a stage and confirm that a previous lesson was thoroughly understood. Problems that are encountered with so called 'trained horses', such as being bad in traffic, refusing to enter water, being very stiff on one rein, or difficult to shoe and clip, can be traced to incorrect or insufficient basic training. An investment in time, skill and patience made at this stage will usually result in the horse performing better, staying sounder and enjoying a longer useful life.

4 Continuation Training

Depending on his maturity and the age at which he was backed, the young horse will either be turned out to grass to mature further, or his ridden training will continue after backing. If he is to be turned away he should continue to be handled and lunged or long-reined occasionally to keep him ready for further ridden training when the time comes.

Hacking

If his ridden training is to continue, it should follow a logical plan. Once he can be ridden off the lunge he can continue his training by being hacked out with another trained horse or horses. This will help to give him confidence in the outside world, although this training will have been started in hand as a yearling. In the company of a trained horse his natural herd instinct will show. He is more likely to follow a trained horse into a strange place than to lead the way himself. In this work he can be introduced to traffic but great care must be taken. Riding horses on the road is a very serious problem, fraught with dangers over which the trainer has little control. The horse must be trained to go in traffic, undesirable though this may be, but the inherent dangers should never be underestimated.

Whilst in the company of another horse he can be introduced to water following close behind an experienced horse through a shallow stream. No opportunity should be lost to walk the young horse through a puddle particularly if he shows a natural reluctance to do so.

There are many other 'hazards' that may frighten the young horse: the pig farm is notorious for some reason; plastic bags in the hedge; milk churns on a stand; washing flapping in the breeze and children on bicycles are some every-day occurrences which he must get used to. If he shies on encountering a hazard, he should be patted on

Fig 26 The young horse should be introduced quietly to 'alarming' objects at an early stage in his training

the neck and allowed to pass it at a distance that seems safe to him. The next day he may go a little closer, and on the third day closer still, until he cures himself of the problem. If he is bullied, kicked or whipped when he shies, it will only compound the problem. By 'association of ideas' he will connect the occasion with the reprimand that he got for shying and the situation will be made worse (see Fig 26).

Out in the countryside he can be introduced to going up and down steep slopes. The rider should treat these as he does a jump, leaning the upper part of the body forward, taking more weight on the stirrup irons and the knees, allowing the horse the use of his back (see Chapter 5). Opening and closing gates is an important lesson that can be taught here. The horse must learn to stand still, parallel and close to the gate with his head towards the latch, whilst the rider undoes it. He must then move away from the rider's leg to enable the gate to be opened, pass through and then stand quietly, parallel to the gate, head towards the catch once again, whilst it is closed and fastened. It is a simple exercise which the well-trained horse must be taught.

Whilst hacking out, much of the work that is done in the school can be practised and in some cases it will be of a higher quality due to the increase of impulsion that is often found outside.

An important aspect of the horse's training, that can only be taught in the open, is galloping. His other basic paces can usually be developed in an enclosed arena or an indoor school. It is best to teach him to gallop in company with another horse that will gallop without pulling and pull up when asked to do so. The young horse should not be allowed to get the idea that galloping is racing, and that he can take charge. It is physically demanding on the horse both on his legs through the effects of concussion and on the heart and lungs due to the extra strain put upon them. In the beginning he should only be asked to gallop a short distance. Perhaps, whilst cantering, he can be asked to gallop on for about 400m (440yd), being pulled up slowly back to trot, and thence to walk on a long rein. As his strength and wind improve he can be asked to do more. The astute trainer will know when his horse tells him that he is ready to do more. Forcing a young horse to gallop more than he is ready for, may shorten his useful life considerably. Finding an area to gallop on is not easy. If access to the downs where racehorses are trained can be obtained then this is ideal. Unfortunately this luxury is seldom available. It is essential that the going is fairly soft, without being too deep. Hard going is bad for the joints and tendons. Young, developing bone is very prone to the effects of concussion and can lead to the formation of splints. Deep going holds the foot and may have a wrenching effect on the young joints and tendons. If an area can be found on which to gallop which is slightly uphill this is ideal. It encourages the horse to engage his hind legs and come off the forehand which discourages him from leaning on the rider's hands and pulling.

When the young horse is hacking out well, in the company of a trained horse, he must start to be ridden out alone. It is a result of very bad training when a horse refuses to leave the others and work on his own.

Leading Out

There are times when it will be necessary for the horse to be led out on exercise from another horse. This does not come easily to all but if his basic handling has been well done and he has been led correctly in walk and trot from both sides, little trouble should be encountered. Whichever method is employed to lead him, it must be safe, effective and conform to the correct principles of training. Fitting a lungeing cavesson and a short lead rein is best as it is safe, effective and conforms to the correct basic principles of training. A well-trained horse can be led by simply fitting a snaffle bridle and taking the reins over his head. This method is safe and effective, other than in a serious emergency, but the action of the bit on the horse's mouth will be incorrect. This is sometimes varied by taking both reins through one bit ring. More control is available this way but the nutcracker action of the bit will be severe and its action on the bars of the mouth incorrect. Many horses can quite easily be led on a stable headcollar, but there will be little control in an emergency. The stable headcollar is designed to tie the horse up in the stable and does not really provide sufficient control to lead him in it in all circumstances. If

Fig 27–9 Correct mounting: stages 1, 2 and 3

this method is used, a knot should be tied in the end of the lead rope to prevent it slipping through the leader's hand. When horses are shown in hand, a chain coupling is sometimes used on the end of a lead rein with a spring hook on each branch of the chain, these hooks are then attached to the rings of the bit. Whilst this affords good control, great care must be taken in its use, as the effect of the bit on the horse's mouth can be severe.

The well-trained horse can be led from both sides but when riding and leading, the led horse should always be on the near side for obvious reasons of safety when riding on the road. Above all, the led horse must be trained to keep up with the leader, control is soon lost if the led horse is allowed to hang back.

Mounting and dismounting for the leader can sometimes present a problem. If this is envisaged it is best to have an assistant to hand over the horse to be led once the rider has mounted. The rider should carry a whip but it should be held in the outside hand where it can be used (not between the two horses).

Schooling

The young horse's training must include working in close proximity with others. If he has been out at grass with other horses during the first years of his life, then this should not present a problem. If he has not, then it will be necessary to introduce him to the situation where he will be surrounded by others, for example, in the hunting field or the collecting ring at a show. This should be done gradually as the young horse, without preparation, plunged into this situation may become excited and be an embarrassing danger to the others.

His programme should include regular periods of schooling in a marked-out arena. This is best done in an indoor school which provides a controlled environment, free from distractions and protected from the weather. When this is not available, then a small paddock or a marked-out arena in a field will suffice. Basic schooling can be done in an open field, but an accurate, marked-out arena makes it easier for the rider to measure what he is doing and ride the schooling figures more accurately. An area 40 × 20m (44 × 22yd) is the minimum size suitable for this work. The going should be good: sand, wood shavings or one of the specialist surfaces are all acceptable but they vary according to the weather and the skill used when they were constructed. Grass is adequate but may be too hard in the summer, frozen too hard in winter, or it is often too wet and slippery. When grass is ideal, a track is soon made by the horse which becomes permanent and difficult to repair.

The purpose of this schooling is to provide the elementary gymnastics that are required by any athlete. It can be compared with the compulsory figures that the ice skater is required to make, the basic steps and positions that the dancer has to learn, or the preparatory work that any athlete, boxer or footballer does in the gymnasium. The intention is to improve the horse's balance, agility, suppleness, co-ordination and strength. He requires these qualities to enable him to carry out the demands of any equestrian discipline whilst carrying a rider on his back. Together with the physical aspects of this work, there is the important element of the establishment of the horse and rider relationship, in which the rider clearly explains what he wants the horse to do and by repetition and reward, he encourages the horse to co-operate willingly.

In all his work the trainer should be striving for the fundamental requirements of the well-trained riding horse. They are that he should 'go forward, be straight, and calm':

1 Go forward means more in equitation than progressing in a forward direction by putting one foot in front of the other. The whole physical and mental purpose of the horse must be to want to go forward with willing energy and impulsion. When considering the requirement of the horse to go forward the question of 'impulsion' must be included. Impulsion is the energy that is created by the hind legs and the hindquarters, it is transmitted through a supple back and received in the rider's hands through the bit and the reins. It must not be confused with speed. The horse can be working with maximum

Fig 30 This horse is above the bit. The back is hollow, the neck and jaw tense

impulsion but hardly going forward at all, as in 'piaffer', (trotting on the spot).

2 Straight means that the horse is not avoiding doing what he is being asked to do by being crooked in some way. To avoid truly using his hind legs he may swing the quarters out to the left or the right. When turning he may bend his neck too much to the left or the right causing the rider to lose control of the outside shoulder. Straightness has a rather specialised meaning here: it also means that the horse should be bent, as much as his physique will allow, on the circumference of the circle on which he is working, or the circumference of the quarter circle that he makes when turning or making a corner. It is not possible for the horse to bend uniformly throughout his length, as there is little or no bend through the rib-cage (see Chapter 1). The main priority in the early stages of his training is that he should be looking towards the direction in which he is going without excessive bend in the neck. Certainly

Fig 31 The horse is 'overbending'; the poll is no longer the highest point of the horse

he must not be bent away from the direction in which he is working.

3 Calm means that the horse should go quietly, without excitement, tension or resistance. The horse in his natural state is a timid, highly strung animal. His sensitivity is one of the qualities that makes him such a rewarding animal to train. This sensitivity must not be destroyed but channelled by careful training to enhance his work.

Consideration must be given in this work to the horse's acceptance of the rider's weight and the bit, without resistance. The natural reaction of the untrained horse, when a rider sits on his back, is to raise the head and croup and hollow the back. This is an obvious reaction when the structure of the horse's back is considered, together with the fact that when he is alarmed he raises his head to look around him. In his schooling he must be encouraged, at first, to lower his head and neck and raise his back, lengthening the 'top line', ie, the line from the poll, down the crest,

Fig 32 Medium walk. Three feet are clearly on the ground, the right hind being lifted to take the step

along the back and over the loins, to the croup and the tail. The importance of achieving this is twofold. Firstly you should instil confidence and relaxation in the horse. He must be sufficiently confident in his surroundings not to be on guard with his head in the air. Secondly, it will help to develop the muscles of the neck, back, loins and hindquarters in a way that will enable him to carry himself and a rider in a naturally correct outline. To this end, each schooling session should be started in walk, with work that encourages the horse to stretch his head forward and down. The reins should be let out long, but with a contact, the hands lowered and the horse ridden forward from the leg. When in walk, he stretches forward and down, with the nose and not the poll the most forward point, the work should be continued in trot and then canter. The aim must be that each time the rider releases the reins the horse automatically stretches the head and neck forward and down in all the basic paces. All schooling sessions should be started and finished with a few minutes of this work to establish or confirm the animal's willingness to accept the bit and the rider.

The paces
Schooling should include continued work on establishing and improving the basic paces.

Walk   In walk, the horse must make long, generous, even deliberate steps in a steady four-time rhythm. It should be purposeful, and he should look as though he is going somewhere. He must walk using his whole body: the head; neck; shoulder; elbow; knee; back; loins; croup; hips; stifle; hock and tail should all move. The walk that appears to come from the elbow and the stifle downwards, with no movement in the rest of the body, is a poor walk. The horse with a good natural walk is often a good athlete and the naturally poor walk is very difficult to improve. It is probably true that the walk is the most difficult pace to improve and the easiest to spoil. Since work in trot and canter may be more exciting there is a possibility that the walk may be neglected.

It is a pace of rest when both the horse and rider are having a break from work, which may mean that standards are allowed to slip. This is particularly so in the free walk on a long rein where the horse is often allowed to idle. In this pace, whilst he is allowed to stretch forward and down and relax the neck and the back, the quality of the walk must be maintained in that he must still go straight with long deliberate strides. It is particularly important in walk that the rider allows the horse to walk correctly. Stiff set hands and arms will discourage the swing of the head and neck and spoil the pace. Similarly a rigid rider will discourage the swing in the horse's back. The rider must allow the nodding of the head whilst keeping the rein contact and allow the swing of the back through being supple in the hips and soft in the waist.

Trot In trot, the horse must spring lightly forward in a steady, two-time rhythm. The steps should be even and regular in length, the head still, the back soft and swinging and the tail relaxed. The horse should work in a regular tempo (see Chapter 7). The rider can either sit to the trot or rise. It is easier on the young horse's back if the rider works in rising trot. Sitting trot can be introduced when the horse's strength, outline and acceptance of the bit are becoming established. As the horse trots, he springs from one diagonal pair of legs to the other with a period of suspension in between the two when no feet are on the ground. To rise to the trot, the rider lifts his seat out of the saddle as one pair of feet come to the ground, and lowers it again as the diagonally opposite pair come to the ground. It will be seen from this that the seat is on the saddle as one hind leg only is in contact with the ground. The horse finds it easier to make balanced turns and circles if the rider lowers his seat to the saddle as the inside hind leg, and consequently the outside foreleg, are on the ground together. This makes it necessary for the rider to be able to change diagonals, that is, lower the seat to the saddle as either hind leg comes to the ground. This is best done by looking down at the horse's outside shoulder, as it comes back, the outside foreleg and the inside hind leg

Fig 33 Working trot, showing clearly the left fore and right hind feet on the ground together, the right fore and left hind feet raised

are on the ground together. This is the beat on which the rider should lower his seat to the saddle. If he looks down at the outside shoulder and counts 'down' – 'down' – 'down' as the shoulder comes back, he will soon learn to sit 'down, down' for two beats and change the diagonal. Changing the diagonal in rising trot is also important to ensure that the horse develops his physique equally on both sides. Riding permanently on one diagonal may well result in uneven development in the horse.

Canter In canter, the horse should make even, unhurried strides of equal length. A steady three-time rhythm must be maintained. One difficulty that arises in canter work is the horse that wants to go too fast and rushes his work. A quiet attitude must be taken towards this, the rider sitting as still as possible with a quiet soft hand, and using the voice in a soft, reassuring way. Pulling with the reins and fighting the horse will not produce the required result. He should be cantered on a circle, perhaps with the weight taken off the seat a little to encourage him to relax.

The horse that is asked to canter too slowly, without sufficient impulsion, may lapse into a four-time canter, where the diagonal pair of feet that should come to the ground together are divided. This is a serious fault and the horse should be ridden forward with energy to rectify it. In the disunited canter the horse has lost his balance and the correct sequence of footfalls, ie, the pair of feet that come to the ground together are on the same side of the horse. This should not occur in the correctly prepared horse, but when it does, he must be brought back to trot, and the canter started again from a well-balanced trot giving him the best possible chance to make a good transition. Some horses favour a particular canter lead and may find it difficult to strike off on a given lead. This is usually due to poor basic training and may prove difficult to cure. Once it has been established that the canter aids are being given correctly and the strike-off is still not correct, the transition should be attempted from a 10m circle, this often helps to solve the problem. Failing that, a cavalletti set at its lowest height, bisecting the angle of the corner where the transition is to be made, sometimes helps in obtaining the correct strike off. When the young horse has difficulty in cantering in an arena due to his size, lack of co-ordination or balance, it is often useful to work on his canter training outside.

If a long, sandy track can be found which goes slightly uphill, this is ideal. The rider should shorten his stirrups about two holes from his schooling length, lift his seat out of the saddle, putting more weight on the knees and the stirrup irons. With a sure rein contact he should then let the horse canter uphill along the track, finding his own rhythm and balance. Once the canter has been improved in this way it can be attempted again in the school but the trainer should not be reluctant to take the horse out again to work on the canter.

Balance
To establish good basic paces the horse must be well balanced, supple and agile with good co-ordination.

In the wild, the horse is perfectly balanced, but clearly, when a rider sits on his back that natural balance is upset. The horse becomes well balanced when he can respond instantly to the aids whilst carrying the rider on his back. If he has little engagement of his hind legs and too much weight on the forehand, his mobility is impaired. If he has too much impulsion but is not allowed to go forward, then he rears up and is out of balance. A well-balanced horse works with impulsion to match the speed at which he is moving. A horse that is trotting fast but with little impulsion (insufficient engagement of the hind legs) is on his forehand and out of balance. The horse that is driven with great impulsion but not allowed to go forward, rears up and is out of balance. There is, therefore, a relationship between impulsion and speed that results in a well-balanced horse. As his training progresses he can cope with more impulsion until the advanced horse, full of impulsion, can make piaffe, levade and the airs above the ground without losing his balance.

To keep the horse in balance the rider must master the use of the half-halt. In this exercise the rider, with the fingers of the outside hand, checks the speed of the horse, asking him to slow down. At the same time he gives quick aids with the inside leg, just behind the girth, to tell the horse to keep springing along, or to increase the impulsion. The half-halt is a rebalancing exercise that adjusts the speed and the impulsion, to match one another, resulting in the horse paying attention and improving his balance. It can be used at any time but is particularly useful before transitions and changes of direction. It helps to get the horse 'between the leg and the hand', which is an important concept in correct riding. It means that the rider has created the impulsion with the legs and the seat and is receiving and controlling it in his hands in such a way that he can speak clearly to his horse and influence his work.

Suppleness
Suppleness is a quality required by any athlete. It means that the muscles and joints are able to be used, free from the restraints caused by stiffness or disuse. Suppleness in the horse has to be worked on just as it must be with the human being. Muscles and joints that are left unused stiffen up and lose their elasticity and flexibility.

Stiffness (the absence of suppleness) is found in the horse due to the lack of elasticity and flexibility in the muscles and joints. It can be improved upon by physical exercise. Stiffness may also be the result of tension or resistance which can only be relieved by careful schooling and horsemanship.

The initial work in hand and on the lunge is the beginning of making the horse supple, particularly if he has been worked equally on both reins. Most horses work more easily on one rein than the other, giving rise to the expression that a horse has a 'stiff side' and a 'soft side'. It is interesting to note how many horses are stiff to the right and softer to the left. Many reasons are put forward to account for this, but the almost certain cause is that they are handled, in general, from the left. They are mainly led from the left, tacked up from the left, grooming is started on the left and they are mounted from the left. The result of this is that the horse tends to bend towards the rider, trainer or groom who is on his left-hand side. If this work was done equally to the left and the right there might be fewer 'one-sided' horses.

If he is noticeably stiff on one rein, it is a mistake to work him predominantly on that rein in order to soften him. The major part of his work should be on the rein that he finds easier. As the work progresses on that rein, it should be changed to the stiffer side. When some small progress has been made on the stiff side, and certainly before any deterioration begins, he should be taken back onto the easier rein. He may never be equally soft on both reins but excessive work on the stiff rein will only set up resistance and may cause physical damage.

The most common and noticeable area of stiffness is in the back muscles, just behind the saddle. Stiffness here discourages the horse from bending left and right and makes the ride uncomfortable. This stiffness may be caused partially by a stiff rider or one who sits too heavily. The importance of soft, supple riding will be appreciated here. Correctly ridden turns, circles, serpentines and transitions will help to increase suppleness in the horse's back.

Agility and good co-ordination come easily to the horse in the wild, but both tend to be upset when the horse is asked to carry a rider. Correct, thoughtful riding will help, together with transitions, lateral work, gymnastics and jumping, all of which will be covered in this chapter.

Work on the circle
Turns, circles and serpentines are elementary school figures that will not only help improve the horse's suppleness, balance and agility, but are practical movements that he will be required to make whilst hacking, show jumping, hunting, playing polo or whatever his future is to be. They are closely related in their execution. The horse is asked to turn by the rider inviting him to do so with intermittent squeezes with the fingers of the inside hand. The inside leg is kept at the girth to maintain or increase the impulsion as required. The outside leg is ready to be drawn back to prevent the hindquarters from swinging out, should this be necessary.

The turn should be ridden as a quarter of a circle and

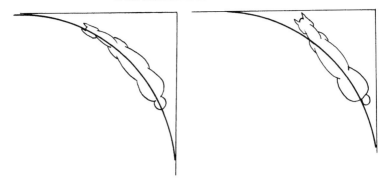

Fig 34 The correct bend through the corner
Fig 35 Incorrect bend through the corner

as the work improves the diameter of the quarter circle can be made smaller, but not at the expense of the horse's balance or rhythm. The corner must not be made so 'tight' that the pace at which the horse is working is spoiled. At first, the corner may be a quarter of a 20m (22yd) circle. As the horse progresses, it can be reduced gradually down to a quarter of an 8m (8³/₄yd) circle. Only in collection is the horse asked to make a corner as a quarter of a 6m (6¹/₂yd) circle.

The aids to make a circle are an extension of those used to make a corner but they are continued, as necessary, until the circle is complete. The horse should be bent in the direction in which he is going and the rhythm should remain regular. A common fault is that the horse bends his neck to the outside and falls in on the circle. This is usually due to stiffness and will improve as suppleness improves. The situation can be relieved if clear leg aids are given with the inside leg, encouraging the horse to bend around that leg. Whilst maintaining the outside rein contact short intermittent squeezes should be given with the fingers of the inside hand to encourage the horse to bend in that direction. It also helps in this situation if the rider can think towards riding shoulder-in on the circle (see Chapter 7). This will help the horse to adopt the correct attitude and is a very good straightening and suppling exercise.

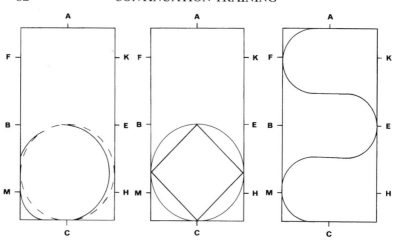

From left to right:
Fig 36 The dotted line shows a good 20m circle, the solid line a poor one
Fig 37 Changing from a 20m circle to a square
Fig 38 A three-loop serpentine starting at A and finishing at C

If the horse bends his neck to the inside there is a possibility that the control of the outside shoulder will be lost and he will fall out on the circle. The trainer must take care, in the early stages, that the horse does not evade the exercise by bending his neck more than the bend in the rest of his body. When riding circles, it often helps to ride them as four separate quarters. The circle must be geometrically accurate with no corners nor flat sides. If the 20m (22yd) circle is ridden in one half of a 40x20m (44x22yd) arena, the rider should aim to use the track, at three points on the circle, as tangent points riding the same number of steps on each quarter of the circle. For instance, the average horse, in trot, will take about twelve steps on each quarter of a 20m (22yd) circle. If, on one quarter, this goes up to fourteen or fifteen steps, the horse has made a corner. If it goes down to nine or ten steps, he has cut across one quarter of the circle.

As his work progresses the diameter of the circles in walk and trot can be reduced down to 18, 16, 14, and 10m ($19^3/_4$, $17^1/_2$, $15^1/_4$ and 11yd) by gradual progression. From time to time the horse must be 'asked' if he can make the circle a little smaller. If he can, without losing his balance or rhythm, then all is well. If either of these qualities is lost, he should return to the larger circle to re-establish them. The 20m (22yd) circle, or slightly less, is the most that should be asked from the young horse in canter although later in his career smaller circles will be required. In trot, the initial work on the circle should be made rising, but as the circle is brought down to 15m ($16^1/_2$yd), or less, rising trot becomes difficult and the rider will find it easier to sit. Great care must be taken at this stage to ensure that the sitting trot is soft and supple and not adding to the horse's difficulties.

Serpentines are an exercise in balance, suppleness and agility in which the horse is asked to join together a series of half circles with a change of rein. It is important that the horse is asked to change the bend before he changes direction to prevent him falling, incorrectly, onto the new rein. It helps, initially, to make the serpentine loops slightly 'pear shaped'. These loops are best made, at first, by joining

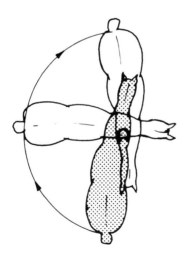

Fig 39 The turn on the forehand

two half 20m (22yd) circles together with a change of rein. Later three serpentine loops can be made in a 40×20m (44×22yd) arena (see Fig 38).

To provide variety in the work during elementary education, there are a variety of school figures that should be attempted. They are variations on the basic theme each presenting a different problem.

Turn on the forehand

Further exercises that improve the horse's physical capabilities and his ability to respond to the rider's requests are those that encourage him to go sideways and forwards at the same time. They improve balance, co-ordination, agility and responsiveness.

The first occasion on which the trainer asks the horse to move sideways is in the stable when he says 'over' and puts his hand firmly on the horse's quarters. This willingness to move the quarters across from a voice aid, combined with a touch of the hand, is an important start.

The first mounted exercise is the turn on the forehand, where the horse is asked, from halt, to turn round through 180° in either direction (see Figs 39–43). This exercise must be made with forward impulsion and any tendency to step

Fig 40–43 The turn on the forehand to the left

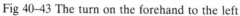

back must be discouraged. The turn on the forehand to the right is made from a square halt, when the rider, sitting correctly in the bottom of the saddle, asks the horse to bend slightly to the right by taking the right hand out a little to that side. It helps if the finger nails are turned upwards to discourage pulling back with the hand. The contact is kept with the left hand to discourage the horse from stepping forward, and the left leg is kept in contact to discourage him from stepping back. With the body weight equal on each seat-bone (ie without leaning to the right), the right leg is taken back behind the girth to ask the horse to move his hindquarters round. On completion of the turn he should be ridden energetically forward to maintain the forward impulse of the exercise.

In the early stages, it may be an advantage to ride through a 90° turn only, until the exercise is understood. The aids for the turn to the left are the opposite to those for the turn to the right. In this exercise the horse pivots around his inside forefoot, making a small half circle with the outside forefoot. The hind feet make a half circle, the radius of which is the distance between the forefeet and the hind feet. To maintain the forward impulsion in this exercise and to relieve any possibility of the horse stepping backwards, it is sometimes made from walk, and is

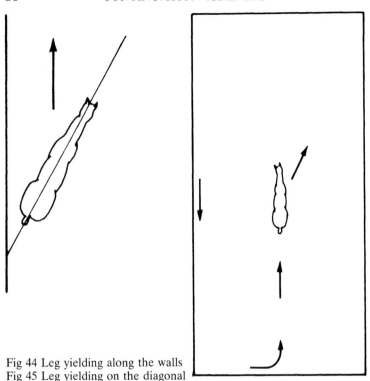

Fig 44 Leg yielding along the walls
Fig 45 Leg yielding on the diagonal

referred to as 'the turn about the forehand'. The aids that are used are virtually the same, except that the horse is allowed to walk forward by the outside hand. Maintaining the true four-time beat of the walk, the forefeet make a small half circle and the hind feet cross over each other to make a half circle, completing the turn. Apart from being good physical training for the horse, it is a useful exercise to help the rider to use a tactful blend of aids. The turn on the forehand has its practical uses opening gates, or, turning in a confined space for instance.

Leg yielding
The logical follow-on to the turn on the forehand is leg yielding. This exercise is made first in medium walk and later in working trot (see Chapter 7). The horse is required

to move forwards and sideways at the same time, the inside legs passing and crossing in front of the outside legs. It is best made by turning down the centre line of the arena, and whilst keeping the horse quite straight and parallel to the side, asking him with the inside leg used just behind the girth to step sideways. The outside leg is kept in place at the girth to ensure that he continues to go forward. The dressage rules require that: 'The horse is quite straight, except for a slight bend at the poll, so that the rider is just able to see the eyebrow and nostril on the inside.' It is difficult to bend the horse at the poll without tilting his head which is a fault. If the horse is asked to bend his neck to the inside in this exercise, there is a chance that the outside shoulder will fall away and the quarters will trail. With these potential dangers in mind it is better that the horse should be kept straight. Ultimately he will be trained in half-pass (see Chapter 7). Errors that are made in the leg-yielding exercise may be carried forward into this work.

To provide variety in the work, leg yielding can be made along the side of the arena (see Fig 44) in which case the horse should be straight and at about 35° to the side. A clear transition should be made between going straight and leg yielding, and going straight again. To improve these transitions, as the leg yielding improves, the horse can be turned down the centre line, and when quite straight, asked to make three steps leg yielding followed by three steps straight and three steps leg yielding until he reaches the side and is ridden forward (see Fig 45). Most horses find this work easier in one direction than the other, but it should be practised on both reins with the aim of making them as even as possible.

Lengthening steps
To improve the horse's responsiveness, it is useful to train him to lengthen his steps from working trot towards medium trot and to come back again to working trot. Work on medium and extended paces will be further discussed in Chapter 7. Longer steps are made from greater impulsion. If there is no increase in the impulsion and the horse takes

longer steps, he will do so because he is on the forehand and running which is unbalanced and incorrect.

An effective way to introduce the horse to taking longer steps is to work in trot, and by use of the half-halt, slow him down around the short side of the arena whilst increasing the impulsion. This is probably best done sitting, depending on the temperament and physical capability of the horse. On reaching the start of the long side, the rider should start rising, close both legs to encourage the horse to use his impulsion and lengthen the steps that he takes with his hind legs, whilst allowing him to stretch his head and his neck forward, in order that he can take correspondingly longer steps with his forelegs. If he is not allowed to stretch forward with his head and neck, the steps taken with the forelegs will be restricted and the work spoilt. It is generally agreed that the horse cannot put a forefoot on the ground further forward than the tip of his nose. If he is unable to stretch his head and neck forward he will stretch his leg out in advance of his nose, but will bring it back to put it on the ground. This results in the rather flashy trot, sometimes seen with show ponies, where the sole of the foot is pointed to the front, with the toe in the air. As the foot is carried forward, the toe should point towards the spot where the foot is to be put on the ground.

5 Training the Jumping Horse and Rider

The Horse as a Jumping Animal

In natural jumping aptitude and skill, the horse rates below the antelope, the cat and even the dog. His advantages, however, are his great strength, memory, generosity and his willingness and ability to be trained to carry a man.

His natural style of jumping lends itself to carrying a rider more than the spring of a cat, or the rather hollow, loping leap of a dog. As the horse approaches a jump, in the last three or four strides, he stretches his head and neck forward and down in an attempt to judge his distance from the fence. As he lifts his forefeet off the ground, he raises his head and neck up and forwards. Immediately after this a great thrust is made with the massive muscles of the hindquarters and hind legs which drive the horse up and forwards. In the flight over the jump the good jumper tucks both hind and forefeet well up underneath himself to avoid hitting the obstacle. Some less well co-ordinated horses tip the feet sideways or kick out backwards to achieve this. During the flight, the wither should be the highest part of the horse, his whole outline forming a nicely rounded curve or bascule. As he descends, he stretches his head and neck slightly, and straightens his forelegs to reach the ground, the outside foreleg first, followed by the inside. He lands on the heel of one forefoot, with the sole of the foot flat on the ground. The fetlock joint is flexed to the maximum, as it supports the entire weight of the horse and rider, perhaps over 600kg (1,325lb). As the hind feet come to the ground and he strides away, the head and the neck are stretched forward to his normal canter outline.

The rider's task is to give the horse a well-balanced load to carry, and once he has clearly shown the horse what he wants him to jump, he should sit in

Fig 46 The novice jumper, relaxed and confident

a soft, still balance, and allow the horse to do the work.

A major contributory cause of knocking down a fence or refusing at it is a poor approach. The requirements of a jumping horse are exactly the same as those of a dressage horse. He must go forward, be straight, calm and obedient. If any of these ingredients is lost, eg, he loses impulsion, is crooked or is disobediently rushing at the fence, then he is less likely to jump it economically or safely. The horse that approaches the fence with insufficient impulsion is unlikely to produce sufficient thrust from the hind legs to clear it. A crooked horse approaching a jump will put himself at a disadvantage, in that any energy that is wasted by going other than in a straight line, detracts from his jumping ability. The horse that rushes a fence out of control, usually jumps hollow and in a poor style, which means that he either has to jump higher, which is wasteful, or he hits the jump. Riding into a jump straight, on the bit, at the correct speed and with impulsion, are the fundamentals of good jumping.

The point at which the horse takes off to jump a

fence depends upon the type of fence and the speed at which he is going. If he jumps with a good bascule, the highest part of the curve that his body makes should be over the highest part of the jump. Whilst generalisations can often be proved wrong, it is safe to say that in normal circumstances, the horse will take off in a zone up to the equivalent width of the fence's height plus a half, in front of the fence, eg, if the fence is 1m (3ft 3in high) the horse will take off between 1m (3ft 3in) and 1.5m (5ft) in front of the fence (see Fig 47). At this distance he is neither in the bottom of the fence, which makes jumping difficult, nor standing off too far, which is risky. The steeplechaser jumping a cut and laid fence at full gallop may stand off a long way, but the show jumper, jumping the puissance wall, will get much closer to the bottom of it to take off. These are the two extreme variations of the basic rule.

Training the Jumping Horse

Jumping is part of the young horse's basic training. It will have been started on the lunge and must be continued in his early ridden work. The requirements from the young horse in jumping are exactly the same as those on the flat. He must go forward with energy and be obedient, straight and calm. In the more advanced stages of jumping and dressage, the priorities are not quite the same, but in early training they are identical.

The objects of training the jumping horse are:

1 To build the muscles of the neck, back, loins, hind-quarters, shoulder, forearm and gaskin to give him the strength to jump.

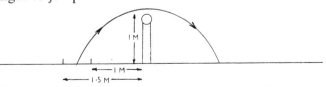

Fig 47 The economical 'take-off zone' is an area in front of the jump between the height and one-and-a-half times the height of the jump

2 To develop his jumping technique by carefully selected exercises.
3 To build his confidence in his rider and consequently make him, the horse, more courageous.
4 To encourage him to enjoy jumping.

Training the horse to jump should only be undertaken by an experienced, competent rider. Lasting damage can be done by a rider who lacks skill, balance or experience.

In all jumping training, the horse should be fitted with boots or exercise bandages together with over-reach boots to protect his legs. Mistakes are often made by the novice horse, and taking this simple precaution may prevent injury that can possibly stop training for weeks. Work on hard or heavy going may cause injury or create lasting blemishes.

To connect jumping to schooling on the flat various gymnastic exercises are started. Not only do these introduce him to jumping, but they improve his flat work as well.

The first exercise is to confirm that he will walk over a

Fig 48 Trotting poles about 1.37m (4ft 6in) apart help to improve balance, agility and co-ordination

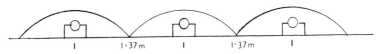

Fig 49 Raised trotting poles at 1.37m (4ft 6in)

pole on the ground. If he was introduced to this as a foal it should present no problems, except that he is now carrying a rider. When he walks over one pole calmly the number can be increased to three. An odd number of poles is usually better than an even number as this discourages the horse from jumping between them two at a time. In walk the poles should be between 92cm (3ft) and 1.22m (4ft) apart depending on the size of the horse and the length of his stride. The distance should be adjusted between the poles to ensure that his natural stride is not interrupted.

When he will walk quietly over three poles on the ground, the work can be repeated in trot starting with one pole and progressing to three. The distance between the poles will be between 1.22m (4ft) and 1.52m (5ft) once again depending on the length of his stride. This work should be made in rising trot, the aim being to trot over the poles in a quiet, relaxed way with energy but without interrupting the tempo of the trot.

When this work is established, the poles can be put in a fan shape on a 20m (22yd) circle. The inside ends of the poles should be about 61cm (2ft) apart, the centres about 1.37m (4ft 6in) apart and the outer ends about 1.68m (5ft 6in) apart. As the horse trots on the circle the poles can be included crossing them at first in the centre where he will take steps of average length. Later, he can be brought in a little so that he takes shorter steps and then taken out a little so that he takes longer steps. This exercise must be done with a soft bend on the circle and without any interruption of the tempo or impulsion.

The next stage is to go back to a straight line and raise the poles about 10cm (4in) (see Fig 49). This encourages him to increase his spring and agility whilst improving his balance.

By this time, out hacking, he will have been jumped

Fig 50 Cross-poles are an inviting, introductory jump

over small logs on the ground, and will have stepped over narrow ditches so jumping with a rider will not be entirely new to him. An inviting start is to place a cross-pole fence at about 30cm (1ft) high, 2.1m (7ft) after a straight line of three trotting poles (see Fig 50). The trotting poles help to concentrate his attention and create the impulsion required to make the jump. This exercise should be continued quietly until he can do it with confidence.

The horse will show when he is ready to go on to the next stage and this will depend on a number of factors. Does he rush or refuse at the fence or knock it down? If his training has been correct these problems are unlikely but it is unrealistic to assume that they never happen. If problems do occur he must be taken back, one or more stages, to re-establish his confidence and obedience. When he is clearly ready to go on, a second small fence can be added, perhaps a brush fence or a rustic spread, a little higher than the first, with 3–3.5m (10–11ft 6in) in between them. He should trot quietly through the poles, jump the first, and without a stride between the two, bounce the second. This exercise can later be extended to give him one stride between the fences of about 5.6m (18ft).

As his confidence grows, more small fences can be added at one stride distance ie 5.6m (18ft), or two strides distance ie 10m (32ft 6in). Each element should be kept low, 45–60cm (1ft 6in–2ft).

This gymnastic work, combined with schooling and hacking out will prepare him to negotiate single jumps. They must be kept low at first, about 60cm (2ft) and be inviting to jump. A small brush fence with a pole over it, a low wall or planks are all good schooling fences. Novice horses tend to jump better if the fence has a good ground line rather than a single pole with a lot of daylight underneath it (see Fig 51). Clear wings, which are at least 50cm (1ft 8in) higher than the jump guide the horse and make the fence more inviting.

In his initial jumping schooling, the horse is ridden into the fence in a steady unhurried rhythm and encouraged to find his own stride with the rider interfering as little as possible. To help the horse find the correct take-off point, it is an advantage to put a placing pole in front of the jump about 2.5–3m (8–10ft) away (see Fig 52).

Fig 51 The steeplechase fence is well filled and inviting with a good ground line

Fig 52 A placing pole at 3m (9–10ft) helps both horse and rider to see the stride and take-off point

Most novice horses benefit from being ridden into their fences at trot as they are less likely to rush and can find their take-off point more easily. If he canters the last two or three steps before the fence, it is unimportant, but more canter strides than this should not be allowed at first.

Once he understands what is required, he should be introduced to the various types of jump that he will encounter in the show-jumping ring. The coloured wall, the gate, planks, a stile, a triple bar and combinations. Care must be taken at every stage though, to see that the horse is not overfaced, ie asked to jump something that is too big for him.

Loose jumping down a lane of fences is an aspect of training that allows the horse to jump freely unencumbered by a rider or equipment. He is free to find his own balance and the carefully measured distances between jumps make his striding exactly right for each obstacle. This exercise can be put up in an indoor school or a secure outdoor manège. The distance between upright fences should be 7–7.4m (23–24ft). From an upright to an oxer 6.6–7m (22–23ft). The horse, fitted with just a stable headcollar and protective boots or bandages is trotted in hand into the lane and released. He should be encouraged to canter down through the jumps with energy but without being bullied or chased. He is caught again at the far end of the lane and rewarded with a pat on the neck if he has done well. The trainer requires one or two assistants to do this work in an orderly way.

Cavaletti are useful equipment in gymnastic training. The safest type to use are those where a pole, about 3–3.7m (10–12ft) is supported by a block at either end. The type that is supported by a fixed wooden cross at each end is potentially dangerous. If the horse hits them they do not roll and an accident may be caused. Piling this type of cavaletti on top of one another, to make a jump, is dangerous and should not be attempted.

In all training it is important to know when the session should end. It is tempting to carry on when progress is being made and the horse is improving. Good work is sometimes spoilt by an enthusiastic trainer who continues past the point when he should have stopped. When some identifiable progress has been made, the horse should be rewarded and the work discontinued.

Common problems
The problems that may be encountered when teaching the horse to jump are:
Refusing This should be avoided at all costs as once the horse has learned to do it, it may never be fully eradicated. It is usually caused by asking a horse to jump a fence that is too big for him or bad riding. If the horse has been overfaced, he must be taken back to a smaller fence and his confidence restored. If he is just being disobedient, he must be reprimanded and re-presented at the fence. The rider must be ready to give two or three slaps with the whip, just behind the saddle, should he hesitate again and to ride him forward from clear leg and seat aids. A training session should never end with the horse refusing. If necessary the fence should be lowered and the horse schooled over it once or twice before he is put away. Advantage can be taken of the natural herd instinct here by giving the horse a lead over the fence. A horse that is refusing will often

Fig 53 The 'V' poles encourage a horse to jump in the centre of the fence and to tuck up the forefeet

jump if he is allowed to follow a trained horse about two or three horse's lengths behind him. It is a psychological error to end a training session on a bad note.

Rushing the fences This can be related to the horse's natural reaction to run away when he is hurt or frightened. If he thinks that he is going to be hurt when he jumps he may well start to rush at the fence. The rider's technique must be good and the tack must be checked to see that it is not contributing to the problem. A poorly fitting bit or noseband or a saddle that pinches or rubs the horse's back may all play a part. The approach to the fence should be made in trot and if the horse starts to rush he should be circled away on a circle of 20m (22yd), or slightly smaller, and kept on that circle until he settles in his trot work. He can then be presented to the fence again, off the circle. This exercise often has the required effect. If he jumps it well he can be brought back onto the circle on the opposite rein and the exercise repeated.

Under these circumstances it may be helpful to change

the approach. The horse may be walked up towards the fence and halted 5–6m (16–19ft 6in) in front of it. The reins are let out and he is patted on the neck and encouraged to relax. The reins are taken up and the horse walked quietly forwards a few steps then into trot and over the fence. There is no immediate cure to this problem and remedies that are reputed to have a quick effect should usually be avoided. Hitting the fence The best jumpers are usually those who naturally tuck the forefeet well up and lift the hind feet well to avoid the discomfort of hitting a heavy pole. There are those, however, who do not seem to mind hitting the poles with their hooves, shins or even the knees. If they do not tuck up their feet naturally, it is sometimes difficult to encourage them to do so. Rapping, ie, lifting the pole as the horse jumps so that he lifts his feet higher to avoid hitting it is dangerous, poor horsemanship, and forbidden by the jumping authorities. Some types of fence encourage the horse to lift his feet, cross-poles are the best example. Placing two poles to form an inverted 'V' on a single pole often has the effect of encouraging the horse to tuck up the forefeet. Any gymnastic work that encourages the horse to jump with a good bascule, and in a good style, should help to relieve this problem.

The Jumping Rider

The requirements of the jumping rider are the same as those of the dressage rider. He must have a deep, supple, well-balanced seat, and an established, correct position. Some successful jumping riders have a rough, unbalanced technique but they are the exception rather than the rule. Suppleness, balance and agility are vital qualities of the jumping rider.

When jumping the stirrups should be three or four holes shorter than when riding on the flat. Exactly how much shorter depends on the rider's length of leg, his saddle and his jumping style. They are shorter to enable the rider to fold the top part of the body forward and maintain his balance as the horse jumps which is difficult to do if the stirrups are long.

When learning to jump it is clearly an advantage to train

on a well-balanced sure jumper whilst the basic technique is established. In his work on the flat the rider will have trotted over poles on the ground so he should now be able to go on to jumping cavaletti and small jumps at 46cm (1ft 6in). To start with fences that are so small that the horse does not really jump, but only interrupts the canter stride, can be at least unhelpful and in some cases dangerous. If there is a fear that the rider may be left behind as the horse jumps and rely on the reins for his balance, he should be given a neck strap, through which he can loop two fingers of one hand to help maintain his balance. If the rider has been trained correctly on the flat, along logical lines, this should not be necessary.

The expression 'the jumping position' is often used by trainers. It may be misleading, as there is no set position that is adopted in jumping, either on the approach, take-off, flight or landing. It is essential that the rider goes with the horse throughout the entire process of the jump giving him maximum use of his body with minimum encumbrance from the rider. The idea that there is a set jumping position may detract from the soft, flowing attitude that is required.

Negotiating a jump may be considered in five closely connected phases: the approach; take-off; flight; landing and riding away. Of these the approach is probably the most important.

Approach
On approaching a fence, the rider must sit in such a way that he can clearly show the horse the obstacle that is to be jumped. He should be able to ride into the fence at the correct speed with the desired amount of impulsion. Under normal circumstances the obstacle should be approached straight and at right-angles to its centre.

As the jump is approached the rider lowers the seat down into the saddle so that he can feel and influence the rhythm of the stride into the fence. Depending upon the speed at which the approach is being made, the body will be almost upright, or inclined forward to a degree, but never behind the vertical. When approaching a fence slowly, the upper body will be almost upright, so that

Fig 54 The good, natural jumper tucks his feet up well

the rhythm and stride can be felt and influenced through the seat-bones.

In racing, or when galloping round a cross-country course, the upper body will be inclined forward, with the seat-bones lowered towards the saddle during the last few approach strides. If the horse is refusing or showing other signs of disobedience when coming into a jump, then it is necessary to bring the body upright, so that the seat can be used strongly in conjunction with the leg aids.

The forward seat approach is usually used in competition jumping. In small arenas, particularly indoors, when the jumps are big and the distances between them short, the expert rider will usually use the upright approach as it is much more suitable to maintain the collection and control that is required in those circumstances.

As the obstacle is approached the hands and arms maintain a sure contact through the reins and the bit to the horse's mouth. If the principle of keeping a straight line from the rider's elbow, down the forearm, through the little finger and down the rein to the horse's mouth is kept, then the rider will best be able to allow the horse to adjust the length of his neck and the height of his head, throughout the entire process of the jump, whilst maintaining a steady but unrestricting contact.

The importance of the position of the lower leg cannot be over-stressed in jumping. The rider who is able to maintain the correct position of the legs will be able to cope with the many emergencies that may arise. If, however, the lower leg position is lost and the leg allowed to swing back or if the knee is straightened and the lower leg pushed forward, then the stability of the upper body is easily lost. It is most important that the ball of the foot is kept on the stirrup iron with the stirrup leather hanging vertically. The ankle, knee and hip joints must remain supple. The heel should be down and out with the toe to the front. It is a mistake to turn the toes out and to grip with the calves.

More contact is taken with the leg when jumping than when riding on the flat but the increased contact should be with the part of the leg between the bottom of the knee and the top of the calf muscle. Gripping with the inside of the knee and the inside of the thigh pinches the rider up and out of the saddle. As the obstacle is approached, the rider squeezes with both legs, in rhythm with the stride, to a greater or lesser degree. Very little aid is required if the horse is approaching with confidence, but strong, even forceful aids may be required if the horse is backing off or refusing. Under any circumstances, feeling the rhythm of the stride with both legs, gives the horse confidence and helps the rider to feel the approach and take-off strides. This should not be overdone, over-riding is poor horsemanship and usually counter-productive.

Take-off

On take-off the horse makes a massive thrust with his hind legs. In order to stay in balance with the horse the rider inclines the top part of his body forward from the hips not from the waist. The shape of the upper body is maintained with the chest up and out, the hips and shoulders straight to the front, the head on straight, looking upwards and forwards. The degree of the fold depends on the size of the jump and the speed of the approach. A low cavaletti approached from trot will require just enough fold from the rider to go forward with the horse; a parallel oxer at 1.4m (4ft 7in), jumped from a strong canter, will require the rider to fold well forward with his chest approaching the horse's crest. The fold forward should not be exaggerated as this only causes unnecessary movement which makes the horse's task more difficult.

Flight
During the flight over the jump the rider remains in his inclined forward position maintaining the rein contact but allowing the horse full stretch of his neck

Landing
As the horse descends and lands the rider brings his upper body back to the normal cantering or galloping position. To bring the body weight back onto the saddle too early may result in the horse hollowing his back with the result that the hind feet are lowered, possibly hitting the jump.

Riding away
When riding away from the jump the rider resumes his normal position to ensure that the horse is balanced and going forward correctly to negotiate the next obstacle.

Jumping technique
To establish the rider's jumping technique there are a number of exercises that are appropriate. When the rider can negotiate three trotting poles at 1.37m (4ft 6in), a cavaletti can be placed 3m (10ft) from the last pole. The poles encourage the horse to be active and help the rider to feel the rhythm into the jump. At this stage he should incline the top part of the body forward a little as he jumps the cavaletti, care being taken to see that the lower-leg position remains correct, and an allowing rein contact maintained. As the rider acquires the technique to cope with this exercise, a second cavaletti can be added 3m (10ft) from the first. This will give the horse a bounce in between the two requiring the rider to get forward and be supple in the

hips and soft in the waist. This exercise can be built up until there are four or five cavaletti in the line of jumps. This will help with the rider's balance, suppleness and rhythm and establish the correct attitude to jumping a single fence. A line of several cavaletti gives the rider the opportunity to correct his technique as he goes through the exercise. To vary the exercise the cavaletti can be put at 6m (19ft 6in) giving the horse one non-jumping canter stride between them provided that this does not encourage the horse to rush his jumping. Eventually a small fence at about 60cm (2ft) can be placed 3m (10ft) after the last cavaletti. This gives the rider the opportunity to use the technique that he has developed over the cavaletti to jump a bigger fence. The logical follow on from here is to build a more substantial jump, perhaps a staircase fence 6m (19ft 6in) beyond the last jump. This may be the rider's first attempt to jump a proper fence and should put him in the most advantageous position to do so.

To ensure that the jumping seat is being established correctly, this work should eventually be done with the rider holding the buckle-end of the rein in the fingers of one hand, dropping the reins and folding his arms lightly across his chest. He should then do the exercise without stirrups and eventually without reins or stirrups. This work will ensure that the rider is developing a truly correct jumping seat, secure, without the use of the reins or the stirrups to ensure his balance.

Once the rider is competent in gymnastic exercises in a straight line, he should attempt those that entail a change of direction. The exercise starts with three trotting poles 1.37m (4ft 6in) apart and a gap of 3m (10ft) before the first jump which is a single pole at about 60cm (2ft). Jumps 2 and 3 are single poles about 1m (3ft 3in) apart, or wide enough for a horse to pass between the inside wing stands. Fence 4 is an oxer about 76cm (2ft 6in) high with a 76cm (2ft 6in) spread, the back pole being one hole higher than the front pole. The distances between jump 1 and jumps 2 and 3, and between jumps 2, 3 and 4, is 6m (19ft 6in).

The first exercise is for the rider to approach in trot through the trotting poles, jump fence 1, make three strides in canter, passing between fences 2 and 3, and jump fence 4. The emphasis should be on correct riding throughout, with the horse between the leg and the hand.

In the second exercise the rider approaches on the right rein, through the trotting poles, over fence number 1, makes one stride in canter and jumps fence 2.

In the third exercise the rider approaches on the left rein, trots through the trotting poles, jumps fence 1, makes one stride in canter, and jumps fence 3.

Exercises four and five take exercises two and three a stage further in that after fence 2, the rider goes left, takes one stride in canter and jumps fence 4, or after fence 3, goes right, takes one stride in canter and jumps fence 4. The track taken must flow smoothly, if it is clearly not possible to take fence 4, after either fences 2 or 3, then the rider should go straight forward, leaving out fence 4 and start the exercise again.

To vary this exercise the type of each jump can be changed. Fence 1 may be a brush with a pole above it, fence 2 may be cross-poles, fence 3 a gate, fence 4 a wall. As the

Fig 55 The 'corner fence' should be jumped at right angles to the line that bisects the angle of the corner

jumps are made bigger the distances between them should be made longer, to ensure correct striding for the horse.

The next exercise provides a jumping course in a small area, it is a series of doubles with one canter stride between elements. It provides training in jumping combination fences, riding an economical track in between fences, and jumping a fence at an angle (see Fig 55). A most useful aspect of this exercise is to teach the rider to ride in a balanced way between the fences, maintaining the impulsion, keeping the horse between the leg and the hand and changing the bend in the horse as he changes direction. The track ridden in this exercise can be varied as suggested in the figures. The types of fence can also be changed to provide a variety of obstacle that is found in a show-jumping course.

6 Competition Jumping

Jumping with the horse can be divided into two broad categories: show jumping and cross-country jumping.

Show Jumping

Show jumping, at its highest levels, is an extremely skilled aspect of equitation. It calls for great skill and courage on the part of both the horse and rider. Its aim is to test the horse's jumping ability and hence his agility, strength and co-ordination. The fences involved can be very high, the puissance wall sometimes standing at over 2.14m (7ft). Show jumping at more modest levels, however, is a sport that most horses and riders can join in and should be part of every horse's basic training.

Show jumping is carried out in a confined arena, some are very large outdoor arenas, some smaller, as little as 95×75m (100×80yd). Indoor show jumping is sometimes held in an arena as small as 70×30m (76×33yd). The jumps are all of an artificial nature although some are built to resemble natural obstacles. All jumps can be knocked down and faults are awarded to horses that do so. The course is required to be jumped at a speed laid down by the rules and faults are awarded for failing to negotiate the course within the time allowed.

Show jumps

There are four basic types of show-jumping fence: the upright; the spread; the staircase and the water jump or long jump.

The upright fence This fence is without a spread and has no depth. Its one-dimensional appearance makes it less inviting and less easy to jump than a spread fence. Consequently it must be approached with care. The rider should keep the horse well in hand, light in the forehand with the hind legs engaged. The speed should not be too great, probably less than when jumping a spread fence. Most show jumps are built with a good ground line which makes it easier for both horse and rider to see the stride and judge the take-off point.

The spread fence This is a fence with depth, the back part usually being a single pole only. In a square parallel fence, the front and the back elements are the same height, which makes it slightly less easy to jump than an ascending parallel in which the back element is about 8cm (3in) higher than

	⊥	⊥⊥	⊥⊥	⊥⊥⊥
⊥	7.47, 24' 6" 10.68m 35' 0"	7.17m 23' 6" 10.68m 35' 0"	7.02m 23' 0" 10.68m 35' 0"	6.17m 22' 0" 10.07m 33' 0"
⊥⊥	7.47m 24' 6" 10.68m 35' 0"	7.02m 23' 0" 10.37m 34' 0"	6.86m 22' 6" 10.22m 33' 6"	6.71m 22' 0" 10.07m 33' 0"
⊥⊥	7.47m 24' 6" 10.68m 35' 0"	7.02m 23' 0" 10.37m 34' 0"	6.86m 22' 6" 10.22m 33' 6"	6.71m 22' 0" 10.07m 33' 0"
⊥⊥⊥	7.63m 25' 0" 10.98m 36' 0"	7.47m 24' 6" 10.83m 35' 6"	7.32m 24' 0" 10.83m 35' 6"	– –

Fig 56 Combination fences. These distances are recommended for horses on normal going. On very good going or jumping downhill the distances should be increased by 15cm (6in) or so. In deep going or jumping uphill the distances should be reduced by a similar amount. When courses are built indoors 15cm (6in) should be deducted from the one non-jumping stride distance

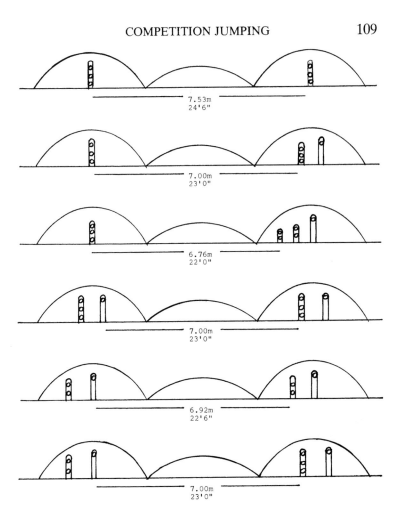

Fig 57 The standard distances found in competition, combination fences

the front. The ascending parallel is more inviting and easier to see than the square parallel. To clear this type of fence well the horse must approach it under control but with plenty of impulsion to give him the impetus to clear the spread. The imaginative course builder will alternate the types of fence to test the horse's ability to go on for a spread fence and come back into the rider's hands for an upright fence.

The staircase fence This is a spread fence in which the front element is on, or very close, to the ground and the centre elements ascend smoothly to the back element which is the highest part. This is the most inviting type of fence as the ground line and the dimension of the jump are easy to see. This helps the horse to judge the take-off point, usually getting well into the bottom of the jump. This type of jump can be taken in a good, forward-going canter.

The water jump This is up to 4.28m (14ft) of water with a low brush fence on the take-off side. The horse is required to clear the entire spread of water with all four feet. This obstacle is usually sited in a way that will allow the horse to approach it at a gallop, or, a very good, strong canter as some speed is required to clear it.

Combination fences Jumps can be made into combination fences consisting of two or three elements with one or two strides in between them (see Fig 56). Each combination is numbered on the course as one obstacle, for example, 2a and 2b, or 7a, 7b and 7c. The course builder measures the distances between the fences very accurately, to make the striding between the elements correct for the average horse. Whilst no two horses are the same, the average length of a canter stride is estimated to be 3.7m (12ft). Only in advanced jumping are the distances varied by the course designer to set a problem for the horse and rider in order to get a result to the competition. The distance between elements in combination fences varies depending on the nature of the individual jumps (see Fig 57). When combinations are jumped downhill the distances are longer as the horse tends to take a longer stride. When the going is deep or uphill the distances are shortened as the strides are shorter in these conditions. The distances are also made shorter indoors as horses tend to be less forward going than when outside. The variations used by a good course builder are very slight, usually between 15cm to 30cm (6in to 1ft) only. The distances are measured from the inside faces of the jumps involved (see Fig 57).

The combination fence is a test of the horse's agility and the rider's ability to keep him balanced and going forward throughout the jump. All combinations should be ridden with a good degree of impulsion and determination. The rider should concentrate on the second or third elements as he approaches the first, which is usually easy to jump. The second or third elements are the real test where problems may arise.

Distance between fences
In a well-built show-jumping course the distance between the individual fences is carefully measured in an attempt to make the course flow easily for the horses and to avoid the riders checking or driving on to negotiate the jumps. In small arenas where the jumps are close together this is very important. In large arenas, where the jumps are well spaced out, it is less important. The course builder will take particular care if there are three, four or five non-jumping strides between two jumps. The distances that he will put between these obstacles will be:

1 Three non-jumping strides: 14.5m (47ft) outdoors; 14m (46ft) indoors.
2 Four non-jumping strides: 18m (58ft) outdoors; 17.5m (57ft) indoors.
3 Five non-jumping strides: 21.25m (69ft) outdoors; 21m (68ft) indoors.

These are known as related distances. When there are over five non-jumping strides between fences, they are considered to be unrelated.

There is a large variety of show-jumping competitions, the rules for which are long and complex. They have a common aim to test the horse's jumping ability, courage, obedience and in some classes, speed.

Cross-country Jumping
This includes the speed and endurance phase of a horse trial, hunter trials, point-to-point racing, steeple-chasing and hunting. Several varying techniques are

Fig 58 The open ditch requires strong riding and the concentration of both horse and rider

required from the rider to ride cross country in its various forms.

Galloping fast across country is considered by many to be the most exhilarating of all equestrian pursuits. Its success and popularity are probably due to the fact that it was an important aspect of cavalry training, and the good cross-country horse has always been in demand for various types of hunting.

The successful cross-country partnership of horse and rider must be able to cope with a wide range of obstacles and conditions that will test their skill and preparation. Not only must they be able to cope with the jumps, but the going, the varying terrain, natural obstacles such as woods, water and the weather all add variations to the task.

The horse's basic training will include hacking out, probably in the company of an experienced horse during which his introduction to cross-country work should begin. Under these circumstances he will be ridden up and downhill, up and down small banks, through puddles and any other available water, over small logs, through the woods and across the plough. These are all aspects of cross-country riding that will be met in competition. In preparation for competition, his training on the flat will continue on a regular basis as will his gymnastic jumping.

As his work progresses training over cross-country fences will start. The obstacles should be small and inviting, starting at about 76cm (2ft 6in), and building up to 1m (3ft 3in). The jumps should be safe (free from any element that could injure the horse should he make a mistake) and on good going, with safe take-off and landing. These schooling fences should be taken from trot and canter, straight at first and then from various angles to develop the horse's agility and confidence. Some work on a loose rein should be included to encourage the horse to be self-reliant and not entirely dependent on the rider for his balance.

This work should all be aimed at building up the horse's confidence. He should, therefore, never be asked to jump a fence that is beyond his capability or that will frighten him. Whilst the work must be progressive, a bad experience at a schooling fence may create a lasting memory that will result in refusals under competition conditions.

Hunting has traditionally been an excellent way of training cross-country horses. It provides an opportunity of riding over country and fences that are not otherwise available and encourages the horse to gallop and jump by being in the company of others. The unexpected, which is often found in the hunting field, teaches the horse to be flexible and resourceful.

Before the serious horse trial is attempted some novice hunter trials should be included in the training. These usually consist of small inviting jumps which encourage the horse to gallop on.

Galloping
Most of a hunter trial or cross-country course will be ridden at the gallop. It is therefore necessary that the horse should be trained to gallop under control and in an economical way. This is a pace in four-time in which the feet

come to the ground in this order: outside hind; inside hind; outside fore; inside fore. To gallop efficiently, the horse must be allowed to use his whole body. The up-and-down swing of the head and neck and the flexibility of the back are essential. Any restriction in these areas will reduce the efficiency of the pace. At gallop, the head and neck may swing up and down through an angle of 30°. The greater the ability of the horse to use the up-and-down movement of the head and neck, the greater his ability to use himself efficiently. The restriction of this swing can reduce the performance by up to 10 per cent.

It follows, therefore, that the rider must sit in a way that impedes the horse as little as possible. Depending on the rider's size and style, the stirrups may be a hole or two shorter than his normal length, to enable the weight to be taken directly off the horse's back and the upper body to be inclined forward. The arm, shoulder and elbow must remain supple to allow the swing of the head and neck whilst maintaining a steady contact. The rider must be ready to lower the seat towards the saddle on the approach to an obstacle where strong aids are required to maintain impulsion and the will to go forward.

The basic paces of walk, trot and canter should be well established before serious work is started on the gallop. This is to ensure that the horse is fit and obedient enough to follow this training satisfactorily. A suitable area is essential. If racehorse gallops are available, then this is ideal. Old turf, going slightly uphill, free from hazards such as rabbit holes or soft patches, is required. In some areas the beach at low tide provides very good galloping, but variations in the going may make it dangerous. Very heavy going risks damage to the joints and tendons, very hard going subjects the horse to the results of concussion, ie splints and strained tendons etc.

At first the gallop should be made well in hand, discouraging the horse from pulling or getting onto his forehand. A suitable plan may be, having found a suitable area, to canter for 600m (650yd), build up into gallop for 400m (440yd), keeping the horse well in hand and to slow down into canter for 600m (650yd). It is important that the horse remains on the bit throughout this work. As his fitness and maturity increase, he can be asked to gallop for longer periods, up to 1,700m (1,860yd) for the novice event horse and up to 6,200m (6,785yd) for an advanced three-day-event horse.

Building up slowly into gallop and slowing down from gallop should be done progressively, abrupt transitions here may well cause injury. The amount of training that is done in gallop must be assessed to suit a particular horse, some require more than others. It is an essential part of his fitness training as it clears the wind and strengthens the cardiovascular system.

Cross-country jumps

These are basically the natural version of show jumps, but include variety that is not found in the show-jumping ring. They consist of upright spread, staircase and water jumps. The character of each of these fences can be changed by the materials used in their construction and the position in which they are sited.

Cross-country fences are usually jumped at a strong canter or gallop. When they are placed in tight or tricky situations they may be jumped from a short canter, trot or even walk. The time allowed for the course, however, is usually estimated at a 'good hunting pace', so time spent in slow canter, trot or walk must be made up elsewhere.

The principle of approaching the various types of fence remains the same, whether in the show-jumping canter or the cross-country gallop.

Spread fences These must be jumped from a strong canter or gallop with good rein contact to ensure that the spread can be cleared. If the horse approaches too slowly or with insufficient impulsion, he will need to make an excessive effort at the take-off to clear the fence. This is uneconomical, a strain on the horse and probably dangerous. He should not, however, stand-off too far at a wide spread as this may give him too much to do with disastrous results. Getting in too deep to a wide spread may also cause

Fig 59 A series of banks should be ridden straight and in a good rhythm

difficulties in take-off. This type of fence is best jumped at right angles and in the centre.

Water obstacles These are popular on horse-trial courses. They fall broadly into two categories. Firstly, where the water is in a ditch, forming part of the fence, and secondly open water into which the horse has to jump.

Where the water has to be jumped, perhaps in an open ditch, both horse and rider tend to look into the ditch taking their concentration from the jump. This type of jump requires positive riding with the horse kept well between the leg and the hand so that his concentration does not wander.

In circumstances where the horse has to jump into the water, careful reconnaissance is required. Most jumps into water are drop fences, this makes the take-off, the depth of the water and the condition of the bottom important. Jumps into water are usually best taken from trot (without loss of impulsion) or a shortened canter. Landing in deep water (up to 60cm (2ft)) on to a soft bottom brings the horse up sharply. With this in mind, he should be brought in under control and on the bit. The rider, whilst not being left behind, should be ready to absorb some fairly sudden deceleration by keeping the leg position secure and the hips and back supple in order to adjust the position of the upper body. Jumps sited in the water and the jump out of the water are best made from trot to avoid splashing that may obscure the jump from the horse or rider and to help maintain balance.

No opportunity should be lost to school the horse through water provided that it is safe.

Banks These should be approached straight and with good impulsion. They are usually inviting obstacles, carefully measured to ensure accurate striding. Where there is a series of banks, or steps up and down, the result will be better if they are negotiated in a steady rhythm. Faltering, or fitting in extra strides, may lead to meeting one or more of the elements incorrectly. The rider should approach banks or steps, which may include a jump, as he would any other combination. When descending banks or a slide, the upper body should be forward in a balanced position. Throwing the weight backwards and standing in the stirrups puts unnecessary strain on the horse. The rider who is in doubt about his balance, in these circumstances, can

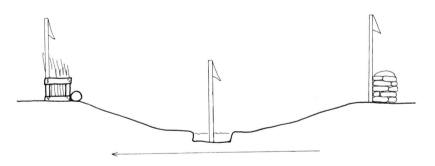

Fig 60 The 'coffin' jump

make a bridge with his reins so that he gets some support from leaning on the horse's neck.

Coffins These are really a form of combination fence which includes a jump, a slope down to a ditch, and a slope up to a jump. They should not present a problem to the horse that can jump the individual elements with confidence. They may, however, take the horse by surprise as he may not at first see the ditch after the first jump. With this in mind the rider should approach the coffin with good impulsion, the horse paying attention and well between the leg and the hand. Determined, even strong riding is often required at these obstacles. The rider should remain supple and in a good balanced position to enable him to go with the horse whilst applying the aids effectively.

Corner fences These are often sited as an alternative to an easier but longer route. They should be treated as a spread fence and jumped at the narrowest point, not too close to the marker flag nor too far in, where the spread becomes very wide. When walking the course careful study should be made of this obstacle, taking note of the take-off and landing and the exact point at which the jump is to be taken.

Steeplechase and brush fences These are designed to be taken at the gallop and are not easy to jump otherwise. They are very inviting fences, usually with a good ground line, filled with brush and built with a good slope.

Hunter Trials
These are intended, as the name implies, to be a competitive test for hunters. The course should be over the type of going that is met in good hunting country, ie grass, plough, moor or heathland. The fences should be natural and inviting, typical of the fences met in a good day's hunting, such as post and rails, hedges, bullfinches, stone walls, gates, ditches and water. They should be inviting, galloping fences for hunters. The trappy, horse trial type of

fence, which sets both horse and rider a gymnastic problem, should not be included in a hunter trial. Some fences can be knocked down to incur faults and as in show jumping a time is set for the course, which, if exceeded will incur time penalties. This time should be calculated at a good hunting pace for that type of country. It is not a race.

The Horse Trial

The cross-country phase of a horse trial, whether it is a one-day, two-day or three-day event, is the major part of the competition. It is designed to test all aspects of the horse's training, strength, stamina, jumping ability, gymnastic ability, courage, obedience and physical fitness.

Each fence is individually designed to test one or more of the horse's qualities. A big drop fence may test his courage, a wide oxer, of solid telegraph poles, his jumping ability and a post and rails in the lake, his confidence in his rider and his obedience.

The length of the cross-country course in a horse trial varies from about 1,600m (1 mile) in a novice one-day event up to a maximum of 6,200m (3.8 miles) in an advanced three-day event. In the novice one-day event the speed required is 525m (576yd) per minute up to a maximum of 600m (656yd) per minute in an advanced one-day event. The maximum speed required in an advanced three-day event is 570m (617yd) per minute. This is less than an advanced one-day event due to the fact that they also have to complete a roads and tracks and a steeplechase course on the same day. These speeds are calculated as a good galloping speed for a horse at the level at which he is competing.

The Point-to-point

This originated as a test for hunters, but is now taken very seriously and only those with a truly professional approach are successful. Point-to-point horses must be 'regularly and fairly' hunted and produce a certificate signed by the Master of Foxhounds to prove it. The horse must carry 79.5kg (12st 7lb). The courses vary in length from 4,800m

to 5,600m (3 to $3^1/_2$ miles). The fences are approximately 1.25m (4ft) high and are brush fences and ditches. Water may be included.

Fig 61 Most cross-country courses include a drop fence where the landing is lower than the take-off

7 Competition Dressage

In the latter part of the sixteenth century the Italian riding academies, that had been the world leaders in the training of horses for many years, began to relinquish that position to the French. As a result European students, visiting the French academies, incorporated French expressions into their own, national, equestrian vocabularies. The word dressage is one of these expressions. At its simplest it means the basic training of the riding (or carriage) horse. Competition dressage, however, puts that training under the microscope and sets tests for the horse, at progressive levels, to examine his natural elegance and ability and the way that elegance and ability has been trained and adapted to carry a rider. Many horses are perfectly well trained to be excellent riding horses, most hunters for instance, but the competition dressage horse requires more detailed, specialised training. The well-trained riding horse must be obedient and pleasant to ride, but with the well-trained dressage horse, careful advanced training returns the natural grace, nobility and character to him that he had at liberty but which is usually lost when he is domesticated and made to carry a rider.

The official definition of dressage, which constitutes part of the rules of competition dressage, is very carefully worded giving a clear, concise explanation of every aspect of the art. This should be read regularly by all competition riders as it is unlikely that they will be successful in achieving their aim if they have not first, clearly established what the aim is.

Dressage horses come from many different breeds, shapes and sizes. This factor alone makes the standardisation of judging very difficult. If, however, the definition of dressage includes the phrase: '. . . the aim is to put the horse in a position where he, the horse, can improve his own *natural* paces and his own *natural* outline, whilst carrying a rider on his back', some progress will have been made towards relieving this difficulty.

The fundamental requirement is that the basic paces shall be pure. (Each pace will be considered in detail later.) The horse must also be submissive. This does not mean that he is defeated and without character or individual personality. It does mean that he is willing and without resistance in all that he is asked to do.

The rules require that: '. . . the horse in all his work, even at halt, shall be on the bit.' The definition of 'on the bit' is clear in the rules:

> A horse is on the bit when the hocks are correctly placed, the neck is more or less raised, according to the extension or collection of the pace, the head remains steadily in position, the contact with the mouth is light, and no resistance is offered to the rider.

If three horses are to be judged in one test, one thoroughbred mare, one Arab stallion and one Irish Draught cross Welsh cob, the judge must have a very elastic view of what 'on the bit' means to apply this rule with fairness as the conformation of each of these horses may be very different.

Straightness is a quality which the rules demand. He must be straight from nose to tail and softly bent throughout his length (or as much as is anatomically possible) on a curve, circle or corner, in the direction in which he is going. The hind feet must follow exactly in the line of tracks made by the forefeet.

In all his work the dressage horse must show lively impulsion or controlled energy which is created by flexing the supple, major joints of the hind legs, ie, the hip, stifle and hock joints. In creating the power to drive the horse forward, the action of these joints lowers the croup, which in turn lightens the forehand, making it light and mobile.

Dressage Grades

Competition dressage is conducted in progressive grades, which in Great Britain are:

1 Preliminary
2 Novice
3 Elementary
4 Medium
5 Advanced Medium
6 Advanced

International dressage competitions are held under the rules of the International Equestrian Federation (FEI). These include:

1 Grand Prix Special
2 Grand Prix
3 Intermediaire II
4 Intermediaire I
5 Prix St George

These are all tests of advanced standard.

The work required at the various stages is as follows:

Preliminary
The horse must show that he has started his basic work correctly. His carriage must be natural and without resistance. He must show that he can make medium walk, working trot and canter, to include a 20m (22yd) circle at these paces. He must be able to make progressive transitions between these paces and show free walk on a long rein and halt.

Novice
He must show that he is starting to work on the bit without resistance. The circles in trot and canter may be reduced to 15m (16$\frac{1}{2}$yd) and half circles to 12m (13yd). Half circles in walk are reduced to 3–5m (3$\frac{1}{4}$–5$\frac{1}{2}$yd). The transitions should become more direct. Lengthening of the stride at trot and trot serpentines are included.

Elementary
Extended walk, collected and medium trot and canter may be included. Circles down to 10m (11yd) in trot and canter. Shoulder-in at trot. Direct transitions from trot to

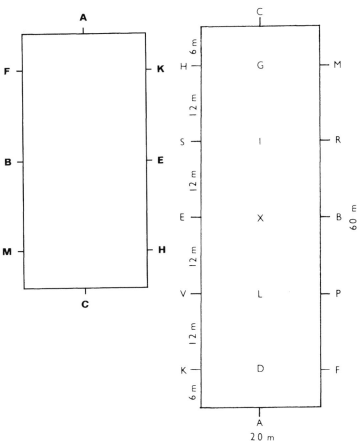

Fig 62 The 40×20m dressage arena used in preliminary, novice and most elementary dressage tests

Fig 63 The 60×20m (international) dressage arena

halt and walk to canter. Canter serpentines to include some counter canter. The horse is required to be on the bit in all his work with the exception of the free walk on a long rein.

Medium
Collectd walk and half-pirouettes at walk. Collection and extension in trot and canter. Transitions from extension to collection in trot and canter. Circles down to 8m (8³/₄yd) and half-pass at trot. Counter canter. Rein back.

Advanced medium
Circles down to 10m (11yd) in collected trot and half circles of 10m (11yd) in canter. Canter half-pass and single flying changes.

The Arena

Competition dressage is held in an arena which is best marked by continuous boards but at times skeleton arenas are used. They are usually set up on grass which varies considerably in its suitability depending on the weather, the levelness of the ground, the length of the grass etc. It is a positive advantage if the arena is set up on suitable sand or some other all-weather surface. Horses work better when they are sure of their footing and the consistency of the going.

The arenas are of two standard sizes, 20×40m (22×44yd) and 20×60m (22×66yd). In general, preliminary, novice and elementary tests are held in the 20×40m (22×44yd) arena and medium tests and upwards in the 20×60m (22 ×66yd) arena. There are few occasions when novice and elementary tests are held in the long arena.

The arenas are accurately measured and are marked with letters (see Figs 62 and 63). These letters and their positioning are internationally recognised.

The school figures required in the dressage tests are based on geometry that fits clearly into these arenas. A 20m (22yd) circle, for instance, fits accurately into one half of a 20 × 40m (22 × 44yd) arena. A 10m (11yd) circle ridden from 'E' would pass through 'X' at a tangent point. It is a condition of the test that the figures and transitions should be ridden with geometrical accuracy, although it will be seen that there are other considerations that have equal and greater importance. The required figure, or transition, should be made when the rider's shoulder is level with the marker.

Equipment

The permitted equipment for competition dressage is clearly defined in the rules. These rules vary, however, between disciplines. The items of equipment that are most strictly covered are the snaffle bit (and its variations), the double bridle, whip, spurs, bit guards and nosebands. Neither boots nor bandages are permitted in any test. (Equiboots are allowed.) No martingale, of any type, is ever allowed in a dressage competition. Competitors are responsible for making themselves conversant with these rules.

The Paces
Competition dressage is:

> . . . the art of showing off the horse's walk, trot and canter to his very best, accentuating the stengths and disguising the weaknesses. The rider is required to prove how well the paces are established by joining them together (transitions), and making turns, circles and various school figures and movements.

A thorough understanding of what constitutes good walk, trot and canter must be established.

The walk
This is a pace in four-time in which the feet come to the ground in the following order: outside hind; outside fore; inside hind; inside fore. The strides should be of equal length, long, deliberate and purposeful. The horse should look as if he is going somewhere. He must walk using his whole body, the head, neck, shoulder, elbow, knee, back, loins, croup, hip, stifle, hock and tail should all move. The walk that appears to come from the elbow and the stifle downwards, with no movement in the rest of the body, is a poor walk. The horse with a good natural walk is usually a good athlete and the naturally poor walk is very difficult to improve.

The trot
This is a pace in two-time, in which the horse springs lightly from one diagonal pair of feet onto the other, with a period of suspension in between when no feet are on the ground. The sequence of footfalls is: outside hind and inside fore together; a period of suspension; followed by the inside hind and the outside fore together. It must

Fig 64 A crooked halt

be free and active with regular steps. The rhythm must be steady, the balance good, with elastic steps originating from well-engaged hindquarters through a supple back.

The canter
This is a pace in three-time. The sequence of footfalls is: outside hind; inside hind and outside fore together; followed by the inside fore which is the leading leg. There

is then a period of suspension during which no feet are on the ground and the stride starts again with the outside hind. It must be light, cadenced (see Glossary) and with regular strides. As in all paces canter must be made with impulsion, which originates in the hindquarters, and is used efficiently through a supple back.

The halt

At halt the horse must stand square with his forefeet and hind feet in level pairs. Equal weight is on each of his four feet. Whilst he must be motionless he must be on the bit and attentive ready to move off instantly at the rider's request.

Variations within the paces

The horse is required to make the basic paces with four variations. These are collected, working, medium and extended. The walk is slightly different in that working walk is not included, but the free walk on a long rein is included in all tests.

Working paces

The working paces are those at which the horse works best. In canter and trot he is active with the hocks engaged and good impulsion. He is on the bit and working without resistance. The pace at which he works best in walk is medium walk in which he takes long, generous steps, over-tracking, ie, the footprint made by the hind foot is in advance of the footprint made by the forefoot on the same side.

Collected paces

In collected paces the steps are shorter and rounder, the neck raised and arched, with the front of the face coming towards the vertical. The joints of the hind leg are all flexed bringing the hind feet well underneath the horse. This lowers the croup and raises the forehand making him light and mobile. Collection can not be obtained until the horse is well established in his working paces. He must be able to work on the bit with good impulsion, and without resistance. Collection is obtained by slowing the speed and increasing the impulsion. There are a number of exercises that help to achieve this (see page 142). Collection must be built up in all three paces over a period, a little at a time. Forcing collection before the horse is ready will only build up resistance and create tension.

Medium paces
In the medium paces the horse takes steps of medium length, longer than in the working paces but not as long as in the extended paces. His whole frame must lengthen, the head and the neck stretching forward to allow a good swing of the shoulder. An increase of impulsion is required to create sufficient drive from the hind legs to lengthen the strides. Medium steps will only come correctly from a degree of collection. If the longer steps are made as a result of the horse going faster, with his weight on the forehand, it will be ungainly and incorrect.

Extended paces
In extension the steps are of maximum length. Impulsion is at its greatest and the horse stretches his frame to allow the steps to be as long as possible, without losing balance or tempo.

In all variations of pace the tempo should remain constant. Collection is *not* made by slowing the tempo as well as the speed and medium and extended paces are *not* made by increasing the speed.

Transitions
These are the changes from one pace to another. A good transition, is where one good-quality pace becomes another without hesitation or interruption. It will be seen from this definition that the transitions can only be good when the paces are good. However, when transitions are carefully made in training, by virtue of their rebalancing nature, they help to improve the basic paces. The aids for making the various transitions were considered in Chapter 2. In competition, marks are given for the transitions included

in the test, which requires them to be ridden carefully and with consideration. They are generally better if they are preceded by sufficient half-halts to ensure that the horse is in balance. This is particularly so in the downward transitions. These are usually more difficult than upward transitions, due to the tendency for the horse to come onto his forehand as he comes down a pace, hence the value of the half-halt to keep the hocks engaged. It is sometimes said: '. . . when making a transition, the first steps of the new pace can only be as good, in quality, as the last steps of the old pace.'

Figures and Movements Included in Dressage Tests

These are designed to prove the horse's paces are correct and that he is balanced and supple. For instance, when the horse makes half-pass in trot, the rider is 'saying': 'Look how well my horse trots, not only can he trot forwards in good balance, but he can trot forwards and sideways at the same time, without losing his balance or rhythm.' The same applies to all the figures and movements. This point is made to stress that it is the *basic paces* that are of first importance and that a figure or movement which is made without balance or rhythm is of no value.

Turns, circles and serpentines

These were covered in detail in Chapter 2. In the dressage tests they must be ridden accurately from the marker demanded by the test.

Dressage Movements

Whilst these must also prove the paces, their well-ridden inclusion in training will help to improve the paces.

Shoulder-in

This is perhaps the most useful and versatile exercise in all equitation. The horse maintains his bend in the direction in which he is going, ie around the rider's inside leg. The horse's inside foreleg passes and crosses in front of the outside foreleg. The inside hind leg is placed in front of the outside hind leg. The rules state that: '. . . the horse

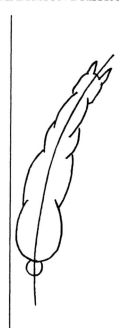

Fig 65 Shoulder-in

is looking away from the direction in which he is moving.'
The fact is, that in shoulder-in to the right, the horse starts
the exercise bent to the right, he makes the exercise bent
to the right, finishes the exercise bent to the right and
continues on the right rein. It is a very good suppling and
shoulder-controlling exercise. It also improves and helps
collection in that it encourages the horse to flex the inside
hock and bring the corresponding foot well underneath his
body. This in turn requires him to flex and lower the hip,
all of which are essential in creating collection.

If the horse is well balanced, working on the bit, and
the turn on the forehand and leg yielding are being satisfactorily made, he can be introduced to shoulder-in. At
first it is best made in walk, to give both horse and rider
time to feel their way into the exercise.

When working in medium walk on the right rein, as the
'M' or 'K' markers are approached, the walk should, by
use of half-halts, be made a little on the collected side of

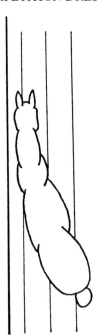

Fig 66 Travers

medium. On reaching the marker an 8m (8³/₄yd) circle is made to the right to create the bend required in shoulder-in. On completion of the circle, as the horse returns to the marker, he should be asked to take the first step on a second circle. As he does this the rider's outside hand checks his progress on the circle and the inside leg, applied just behind the girth, encourages him forward along the track. The inside hand and leg maintain the bend, whilst the outside hand leads him down the track, with a slight opening rein effect, the outside leg being ready to prevent the quarters from swinging out to the left should they tend to do so. He makes three clear lines of tracks, the inside line with the inside forefoot, the centre line with the inside hind and the outside fore together, and the outside track with the outside hind foot (see Fig 65). After three or four steps he should be ridden forward on the circle on which he is bent not taken back onto the track. He is rewarded with a pat on the neck if he has done well. If the shoulder-in deteriorates and balance is lost he should be sent energetically forward on a circle to repair the damage and the exercise started afresh.

It is almost certain that he will find this work easier on one rein than the other but care should be taken to make the work as even as possible on both reins. Many uses will be found for this exercise: it helps with the lengthening of the steps in walk and trot; the transition to canter; straightening the horse who works with his quarters in and preparation for half-pass.

Travers
This is a quarter-controlling exercise in which the horse, whilst bent slightly around the rider's inside leg, takes his hindquarters in from the track, so that he is at about 30° to the wall. The outside legs pass and cross in front of the inside legs. A practical way to start this exercise is to make an 8m (8³/₄yd) circle similar to the start of shoulder-in but on completion of the circle, as the horse's nose and ears are pointing straight down the track, the rider brings back his outside leg and asks the horse to bring his hind feet in off the track a little. He should be making three clear lines of tracks on the ground, the inside line with his inside hind foot, the middle line with the inside fore and outside hind and the outside line with the outside forefoot, (see Fig 66). After three or four steps, initially in walk, he should be ridden energetically straight down the track. This exercise can eventually be ridden in trot. Whilst it is possible to ride travers in canter, care must be taken as the horse frequently evades his work in canter by bringing the quarters in, which is a serious fault. This exercise continues to improve co-ordination, agility and collection and is a very useful introduction to half-pass.

Half-pirouette in walk
This exercise requires that the horse should walk a half circle on two tracks. The hind feet make a very small circle, almost pivoting around the inside hind foot, and the forefeet make a larger half circle, the radius of which is the distance between the forefeet and the hind feet. The

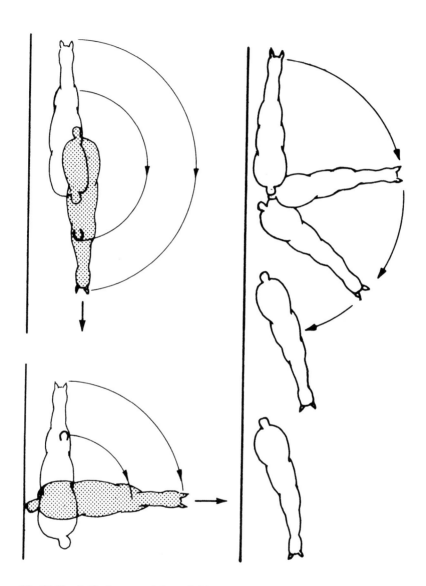

Fig 67 The half-pirouette (above left)
Fig 68 The half-pirouette into renvers (right)
Fig 69 The quarter-pirouette (below left)

four-time tempo of the walk must be maintained. The exercise must be made with impulsion, going forward and with no sign of stepping backwards. The horse remains slightly bent in the direction in which he is going.

There are a number of ways of approaching this exercise. Whichever is used, it should be remembered how easy it is to spoil the walk and that all this work must be ridden forward with energy.

One approach is to make a 20m (22yd) circle in medium walk and to change that circle to a square with its corners at the tangent points of the circle. As the tangent points are approached, the collection is increased by the use of the half-halt. At the corner, the outside hand checks the forward movement, the inside hand, with a slight opening rein effect, invites the horse to turn. The inside leg maintains the bend and the impulsion, whilst the outside leg prevents the hindquarters from swinging out. This is the start of a quarter-pirouette. On its completion the horse is ridden forward in medium walk. The exercise can be repeated at the next corner and so on.

Alternatively, the exercise can be introduced from a 6m (6½yd) volte in collected walk. The aids for making the volte are the same as they are for any circle. As the horse improves in making the volte, it can be reduced in diameter until he can make the first half of the volte into a quarter-pirouette. This is achieved by slightly varying the blend of the volte aids. The inside hand, with a slightly opening effect, has to invite the forehand round on a shorter route. The outside hand, with the rein close to the neck, prevents him from walking forwards on the circle. The outside leg acts as the quarter-controlling leg, remaining at the girth, maintains the impulsion and ensures that the movement is made in a forward direction. On completion of the quarter-pirouette, the horse is ridden energetically forward in walk.

Whichever method is used to introduce the horse to this work, once the quarter-pirouette is established, he can work towards the half-pirouette by continuing to apply the same aids. The exercise should be done as evenly as possible on both reins.

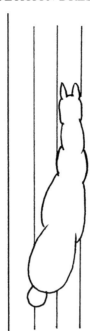

Fig 70 Renvers

Renvers
This is a similar movement to travers, except that the horse's tail is towards the wall instead of his head. Once again the exercise is best started in walk from a half-pirouette. Towards the end of the half-pirouette, and before the fore-hand reaches the track, the rider checks further progress on the pirouette with the fingers of his outside hand. The inside hand and leg maintain the bend and the outside leg, drawn back behind the girth, moves the hindquarters along the wall, the horse's inside legs passing and crossing in front of the outside legs. At the completion of the exercise the horse should be ridden straight forward with energy (see Fig 70). A simple introduction to renvers in trot is to turn down the arena 8m (8³/₄yd) from the track on the left rein. When level with the half marker 'E' or 'B', make an 8m (8³/₄yd) circle to the left. On completion of that circle, and as the horse's nose and ears are pointing down the original track, the rider's outside leg is taken back to control the

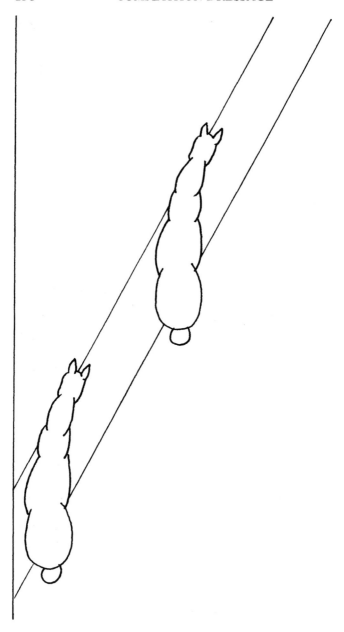

Fig 71 Half-pass

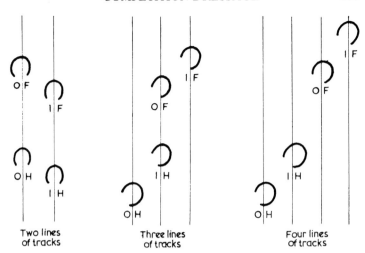

Fig 72 Two, three and four tracks

quarters and the aids are applied in exactly the same way
as they were to make renvers from the half-pirouette in
walk. All this work should be a little on the collected side
of either medium walk or working trot. Renvers should be
practised equally on both reins. Its value is the same as
travers but it is rather more demanding of both horse and
rider as they are without the wall to guide the forehand.

Half-pass
This is the most advanced lateral exercise. It is similar to
travers, except that it is made across the diagonal of the
arena and not along the wall. The exercise must be made
with a fair degree of collection. The horse, whilst almost parallel to the wall, but with the forehand slightly in advance,
takes generous steps equally forwards and sideways. He is
bent in the direction in which he is going. The outside legs
pass and cross in front of the inside legs, the rhythm and
tempo are maintained with good impulsion.

If the preparatory work of shoulder-in and travers has
been well done the half-pass should follow as a natural con-
sequence. It may be started in a number of ways. Starting a
little on the collected side of medium walk, on the left rein,
the horse is asked to make a 10m (11yd) circle from either

'M' or 'K', followed by another half circle, which brings
him back onto the centre line, looking towards 'B' or 'M'.
Maintaining the bend created on the circle with the inside
leg and hand the rider brings the outside leg generously back
to move the hindquarters across, making half-pass towards
'B' or 'M', whilst maintaining the forward impulsion with
the inside leg. At first, on completion of a few steps in
half-pass, the horse should be ridden energetically forward

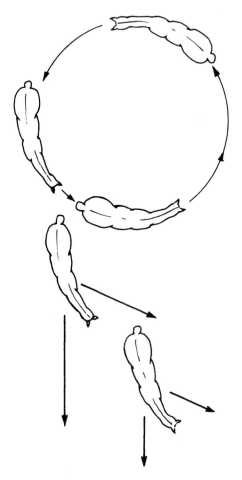

Fig 73 Half-pass from a 10m circle

in a straight line. It is usually a comparatively short time before the work can be attempted in trot.

Some horses find half-pass in canter comparatively easy. If the working canter is well balanced and able to be shortened, this exercise may benefit both the canter and the half-pass in other paces. Canter half-pass can be started by riding half a 10m (11yd) circle from 'M' or 'K' on the left rein and on reaching the 'A'–'C' line making half-pass back towards 'B' or 'E' to change the rein. The aids being the same as those for half-pass in trot.

An alternative method in trot is, when on the right rein for instance, to make a 10m (11yd) circle from 'F' or 'H', followed by a further half circle onto the 'A' –'C' line. Using the bend created by that circle continue down the 'A'–'C' line in shoulder-in right. After four or five steps, when the position of the horse is exactly right for half-pass, the rider's outside leg is taken back to move the quarters across and make half-pass for four or five steps towards 'K' or 'M' (see Fig 73).

Common faults that may be encountered, but should be avoided are:

1 Insufficient or too much sideways movement.
2 The hindquarters leading, usually due to excessive use of the rider's outside leg.
3 Hindquarters trailing, due to incorrect or insufficient use of the outside leg aid.
4 The inside shoulder leading due to incorrect bend in the neck. This may be as a result of incorrect leg yielding when the horse was not kept straight but allowed to bend away from the direction in which he was going.

The rein back
In this exercise the horse steps backwards in a straight line. The feet are lifted clearly in diagonal pairs and are put down together without dragging. This exercise is not confined to the dressage arena, all horses must be able to step backwards, hunters, jumpers or the ordinary hack. In the dressage test, however, he must remain on the bit. Starting from a square halt he steps back the required

number of steps. On completion of the rein back he must go directly forward, without hesitation, in the pace demanded by the test.

To make the rein back, the rider first ensures a square halt. He then, whilst sitting full in the bottom of the saddle with the body upright, closes both legs, just behind the girth as if to ride straight forward, but instead of allowing the horse to walk forward he softly restrains the forward movement with his hands. As a result the horse, with forward impulsion, steps backwards. The rider counts the number of steps that he steps back and on completion immediately applies the aids to ride the horse forward in the required pace.

Lengthening and shortening the steps

To obtain variations within the paces the rider must develop good feel and be able, by correct application of the aids, to have the horse truly between the leg and the hand. He must be able to create the required degree of impulsion with the legs and the seat and receive and control it in his hands. Only under these circumstances will he be able to vary the length of the steps within the pace.

Before medium or extended paces are attempted, work must be done to increase the impulsion by engaging the hindquarters and lightening the forehand, ie increasing the collection. This is based on the fact that a spring must be wound up before it can be released. Attempts to lengthen the steps whilst the horse is on his forehand will result in the horse running and going further onto the forehand.

Collection is obtained by the use of the legs and the seat to encourage the horse to flex the hip, stifle and hock joints and step further underneath himself with the hind feet. This results in a lowering of the croup, which in turn, raises and lightens the forehand. This is only successful if the horse remains soft and supple in the muscles that control the jaw, the poll, the neck and the back. If tension or resistance are created the collection is of no value and the work should be taken back a stage to re-establish the submission and acceptance of the bit. The value of the half-halt will be appreciated here as its purpose is to slow the speed of the horse whilst maintaining or increasing the impulsion. Other exercises that help to improve collection are: the rein back; shoulder-in; travers, renvers and half-pass or any work that encourages the horse to flex the big joints of the hind leg.

Once a degree of collection has been established, lengthening the steps can be attempted. It is best approached by working in a collected pace around the short side of the arena. On approaching the quarter marker at the start of the long side, close both legs and allow with the hands whilst still maintaining rein contact to encourage the horse to take longer steps. The rider must experiment with each particular horse to discover how much leg and how much hand is required to achieve the desired result in either medium or extended paces. The return from medium or extension to working or collected pace should be made through a correct transition, not by allowing the horse to fall back to the shorter pace.

Often progress is made by lengthening the steps from shoulder-in. If shoulder-in is made from the start of the long side, to the first quarter marker, and on reaching that marker the horse sent across the diagonal in the longer steps the work may be improved, due to the collecting effect of the shoulder-in.

Counter canter
Here the horse is required to work to the right with the left canter lead or vice versa. It is intended to show that he is obedient, supple and well balanced. It is one of the rare occasions when the horse is bent away from the direction in which he is going, the neck being bent a little towards the leading foreleg.

To introduce the horse to this work, shallow loops should be made on the long side of the arena between the quarter markers, so that he is about 3m ($3^1/_4$yd) in from the half markers to start with. As his balance and understanding of what is required improve, the loops can be made larger, up to 5 or 6m ($5^1/_2$ or $6^1/_2$yd). The object of the exercise is that the horse should return to the track on the second half of the loop in counter canter. When progress has been

made on both reins, a change of rein from quarter marker
to quarter marker can be attempted, and the horse ridden
in counter canter through the first corner. He should then
be asked to trot before he loses his balance and either falls
back into trot, or changes the canter lead in front and
becomes disunited. Horses will progress at varying rates in
this work. It should not be hurried and only taken a stage
further when the horse shows that he is ready. In counter
canter, it is to the rider's advantage to keep the outside
leg (the leg on the outside of the bend of the horse) back,
towards the canter aid, and to ensure that the bend to the
outside of the arena is maintained with the inside leg and
hand (ie, the inside of the bend of the horse).

The simple change
In this change of leading leg the transition is made from
canter to walk and after two or at the most three, walk
steps, canter is restarted on the opposite leading leg and
the direction changed. It is best to introduce this to the
horse across the diagonal from quarter marker to quarter
marker. A few canter steps before 'X' he is asked to trot,
and as the opposite quarter marker is reached, asked to
canter on the new lead. As progress is made the number
of trot steps is reduced until it is down to three or four.
As the walk to canter transition improves the exercise can
be changed to: canter, trot through 'X', walk three or four
steps, canter. Gradually the downward transition, canter
to walk, can be introduced. It is the most difficult part of
the exercise and should be progressive, through trot, until
the horse is ready to make it direct.

Flying change of leg at canter
In this exercise the horse changes from canter left to
canter right (or vice versa) without interrupting the canter. After the period of suspension in the canter stride the
leading foreleg is determined by which hind leg is put to
the ground first. If the right hind is put down first then
the left fore will lead. If the left hind is put down first the
right fore will lead. It follows that the rider must indicate
to the horse which hind leg he should put on the ground,

after the period of suspension, to make the flying change. The benefits of teaching the correct aids for the transition to canter in the initial stages, will be appreciated here.

Once the walk to canter and the walk to counter canter can be guaranteed at any point in the arena, ie on the long side, in the corners or up the centre line, work can be started on the flying change.

It should be started early in the training session whilst the horse is quite fresh. Some time should be spent on normal warming-up to include the direct transitions, walk to canter and walk to counter canter on both reins.

There are a number of ways in which the exercise can be attempted. The one chosen should be the most suitable for a particular horse or the one that is the personal preference of the trainer.

The flying change can be made by:

1 Changing the rein in canter from quarter marker to quarter marker and making the flying change from counter canter in the corner.
2 Making half a 15m (16^1/$_2$yd) circle from the half marker returning to the track to change the rein and making the flying change on reaching the track.
3 Working on a 20m (22yd) circle and making the change from counter canter on the circle.

First method Changing the rein in canter across the diagonal. The trainer must decide on which rein the horse prefers to canter as this is the rein to which he is going to attempt to change. He then canters half a circuit of the arena on the other canter lead and changes the rein across the diagonal say from 'M' to 'K'. If this work is new to the rider, it may help him to think that he is in sitting trot and is going to ask the horse to canter in the next corner. With this in mind, as he approaches the corner he simply applies the aids to canter left. They must be made deliberately and clearly to ensure that the horse changes behind and not just in front, making him disunited.

The advantage of this method is that the horse is encouraged to change by the corner and he is changing from counter canter on the lead that he likes least, to true canter, on the lead that he finds easier.

The disadvantages of making flying change by this method are that he may learn to anticipate the change and disobediently change each time he enters a corner in counter canter. This often results in him changing only in front and becoming disunited. It also involves the rider in the problems of riding the corner correctly and making the flying change.

Second method Make half a 15m (16½yd) circle from the half marker and return to the track before the quarter marker, making the flying change as the track is rejoined. Once again it should be made from counter canter on the least favoured leg, to true canter on the easier leading leg. In preparation for this exercise, it often helps to start by making a simple change through a few steps in walk as the track is rejoined, reducing the number of walk steps until the flying change is made. The aids for the change should, once again, be deliberately applied to ensure the correct change behind.

Third method Work is started on a 20m (22yd) circle and frequent transitions are made from walk to canter and canter to walk, walk to counter canter and counter canter to walk. When these transitions are sure, the number of walk steps is gradually reduced. Eventually, when in counter canter on the least preferred leg, the horse is asked to make flying change to true canter. The work must remain quiet and calm. The advantage of this method is that the horse is being asked to change his canter lead entirely by the correct use of the aids and there is no reliance on either a change of direction or the horse feeling that there is a logical place to change the lead, both of which introduce an element of disobedience. An added advantage is that the rider has an unlimited number of opportunities to ask for the change. This enables him to give the aid when he feels that the horse is ready, rather than at a given point on the arena.

Whichever method is used, the exercise should not be continued for too long. Once some slight progress has been made, or one flying change has been made, the horse should be congratulated and the subject changed. It is usually counter-productive to continue this work for too many days in succession.

When the flying changes are established, to ensure obedience and balance, it is useful to make them from true canter to counter canter. Eventually, the dressage tests require the horse to make flying change every four strides, then three strides, two strides and every stride. These are known as tempo changes.

The flying change in canter is not confined to the dressage arena, it is a natural movement for the horse to make and is required from the well-trained show jumper or polo pony.

Counter change of hand
This exercise is designed to show how well the half-pass is established together with the horse's balance, agility and obedience. A zig-zag movement is made in half-pass changing from half-pass left to half-pass right and so on. A set number of steps is made without losing balance, rhythm or impulsion. One step may be made straight forward in between changes of direction. Once the horse is capable of making half-pass well on both reins, this exercise should present few problems.

The canter pirouette
This is a very advanced exercise and must not be attempted until the horse can work quietly and calmly in canter with a very high degree of collection. He must be able, whilst maintaining the clear three-time rhythm, to slow the canter speeds right down until he is almost cantering on the spot but keeping good impulsion.

There are a number of important factors to bear in mind when teaching the horse this exercise:

1 The rider must maintain a correct, upright, balanced position.
2 The work is very tiring on the horse and should not be overdone.
3 The full pirouette should be built up through the quarter-, the half- and the three-quarter pirouette.

As in all advanced work this exercise can be introduced to the horse in a variety of ways. It is for the trainer to decide which of these approaches is best for a particular horse.

First method Whilst making a large pirouette in walk the horse can be asked to strike off in canter, make two or three steps in canter pirouette and then be sent straight forwards in canter. If the balance is lost, or the work deteriorates, the horse should be returned to walk and sent straight forward. The walk to canter transition must be of high quality if this method is to be successful.

Second method Half a 6m (6½yd) volte is made in collected canter at the end of the long side of the school. The horse is then ridden down the long side in renvers for five or six paces and the half-pirouette made towards the wall. This method is particularly useful to discourage the hindquarters from swinging out which is a frequent difficulty in this exercise.

Third method It is often helpful to make a few steps in canter pirouette from a good canter half-pass. This is because the bend should be correct, the collection good and the outside hind leg well engaged.

Piaffer

The piaffer is a highly measured, collected, elevated and cadenced trot on the spot. The horse's back is supple and vibrating. The quarters are slightly lowered, the haunches, with active hocks are well engaged giving great freedom, lightness and mobility to the forehand. Each diagonally opposed pair of feet is raised and returned to the ground alternately, with an even rhythm and slightly prolonged suspension.

In principle, the height of the toe of the raised foreleg should be level with the middle of the cannon bone of the other foreleg. The toe of the raised hind leg should reach just above the fetlock joint of the other hind leg. (This is the FEI definition of piaffer.)

Teaching the piaffer to the horse is a task for the experienced trainer only. The exercise is the culmination of maximum impulsion and lightness of the forehand. When the horse is capable of a high degree of collection and can make the transitions from collected trot to halt and collected to working trot smoothly, combined with the ability to make collected walk whilst remaining straight and calm, piaffer can be attempted.

It should first be made in hand, with the horse dressed as for lungeing with the side reins sufficiently short to prevent him bending his neck too much to the left or the right when in his collected outline. This training is best carried out to start with on the track with the horse parallel to the wall.

When working on the left rein the trainer holds the lunge rein with his left hand and a long whip (not a lungeing whip) in his right hand. The horse is worked in collected walk and the speed gradually reduced by the use of the lunge rein which is held up fairly close to the lungeing cavesson. The impulsion is maintained by the trainer tapping the horse lightly below the hocks with the long whip. As soon as one or two steps are made in piaffer, whilst still moving slightly forwards, the horse is allowed to go forwards and is rewarded by a pat on the neck. The exercise should be made with frequent changes of rein.

Once the piaffer is becoming established in hand, it can be attempted with the rider in the saddle. The work is once again made from collected walk, the rider slowing down the speed with the fingers and maintaining the impulsion with his seat and legs. The trainer may still help from the ground by tapping the hind legs alternately just below the hocks in rhythm with the steps. It is very important at this stage that the horse is allowed to go forwards a little as he makes piaffer. Only in the most advanced tests is piaffer required on the spot. It is always better if the horse is going forward a little; he must never step back.

Passage
This is a measured, very collected, very elevated and very cadenced trot. It is characterised by a pronounced engagement of the quarters, a more accentuated flexion of the knees and hocks and a graceful elasticity of movement. Each diagonally opposed pair of feet is raised and returned to the ground alternately, with an even rhythm

and prolonged suspension. In principle the height of the toe of the raised foreleg should be level with the middle of the cannon bone of the other foreleg. The toe of the raised hind leg should be slightly above the fetlock joint of the other hind leg.

This is a very advanced and demanding exercise and is probably the ultimate test of the rider's feel and the correct logical training of his horse. If the horse is working well in piaffer and is willing to go freely forward from it the rider should not find a few steps in passage too difficult. The horse is sent energetically forwards from piaffer by the rider's seat and legs with the hands allowing him to go forwards but at the same time restraining the movement sufficiently to produce the graceful, elevated steps of passage.

It must be remembered that passage requires great physical effort from the horse and only a few steps should be asked for at first. On completion of the few steps in passage the horse should be ridden forwards in collected trot to ensure that this does not deteriorate as a result in the introduction of passage.

In all the training of the riding horse and in particular the more advanced work, it is of enormous value to the rider if he has himself been trained on an experienced horse that will, on the correct application of the aids, perform the task. Whilst it is not impossible the inexperienced rider training an inexperienced horse is faced with many difficulties. However, the use of commonsense and the help of an experienced trainer can produce surprisingly good results.

Riding the Dressage Test

The skilled dressage rider rides the test in such a way that he shows off the horse's strengths and disguises his weaknesses. To do this he must know his horse and the work required by the test thoroughly. As the test requires him to show the movements in a particular order he must learn it so as to be able to remember it in detail under the pressure of competition. It is expensive in marks, embarrassing and shows signs of being ill-prepared to go wrong in a test. It is allowed in some competitions for the rider to have a commander, an assistant who calls out the test as he goes through it but a rider who requires this shows signs of being ill-prepared. Having learned the test, it is a mistake to practise it on the horse too often. The horse's memory and willingness to perform sometimes results in him learning the sequence of movements and anticipating them in the competition. This is undesirable.

The competition dressage test should be ridden with a degree of dash. The apologetic rider who creeps carefully through the test without making a mistake, but without any sparkle, should not gain good marks. The good rider will show his horse boldly, looking the judge in the eye and inviting him to look closely at his horse.

The entry at 'A', the halt and salute are the first movements that the judge sees. They should be bold, straight and made with impulsion. The rider should not remain too long at halt whilst making his salute. It is important that he sits still, maintaining the leg and rein contact during the salute. This keeps the horse square and attentive. Dropping the reins and letting the legs fall away is a sure way to lose the horse's attention. When saluting it is only necessary to take the reins and the whip in the left hand maintaining the rein contact, the right hand is put down to the side and the chin lowered and raised. Gentlemen remove the hat without bowing. Bowing from the waist is incorrect. The salute should not be hurried but it is a mistake to stand in halt at the 'X' marker any longer than is necessary. The same applies to the halt and salute at the end of the test.

The following will almost certainly result in the loss of marks:

1 Riding in an irregular tempo.
2 Incorrect bend in the horse.
3 Failing to ride forward with energy.
4 The horse or rider being crooked.
5 The rider sitting or applying the aids in such a way that it causes the horse difficulties.
6 Failing to change or being erratic in changing the diagonal in rising trot.

7 Any resistance, disobedience, lack of attention or submission on the part of the horse including whinnying.
8 Inaccurately ridden figures.
9 Late or early transitions which are as a result of
disobedience or lack of balance.
10 Stiffness.
11 Lack of acceptance of the bit, ie being above, over or
behind the bit or being overbent.
12 Unlevel steps, whether due to lameness or incorrect
training or riding.
13 Grinding the teeth or swishing the tail.

The following diagrams show common faults that are frequently found at preliminary and novice levels, but may
be found at all levels:

Fig 74 The test requires the rider to 'turn left at E and right at B'. The
dotted line shows a good track, the solid line a poor one
Fig 75 Here the dressage test requires that 'in canter, half circle right
20m between B and F returning to the track between B and M'. The
solid line shows a poor track, the dotted line a good one
Fig 76 The solid line shows the effect of trying to turn up the centre
line from A to finish the test. It is better to follow the dotted line and
ride a half 10m circle from K to D.
Fig 77 Unevenly ridden corners, such as these, will score poor marks
Fig 78 The test requires that 'in medium walk B to X half circle right
10m diameter, X to E half circle left 10m diameter'. The dotted line
shows a good track, the solid line a poor one
Fig 79 Here the rider has entered too close at A and at an angle which
has made it impossible for him to ride straight down the centre line.

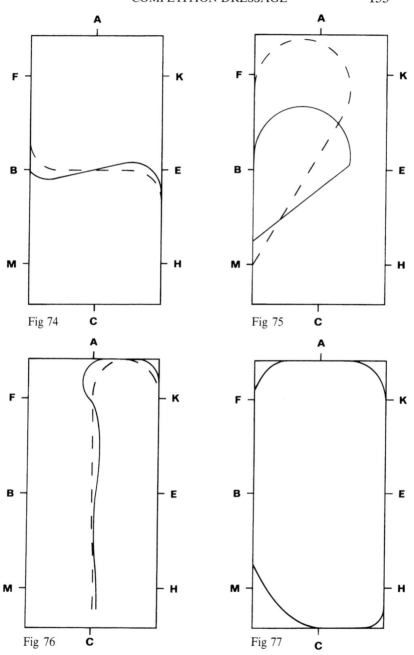

Fig 74

Fig 75

Fig 76

Fig 77

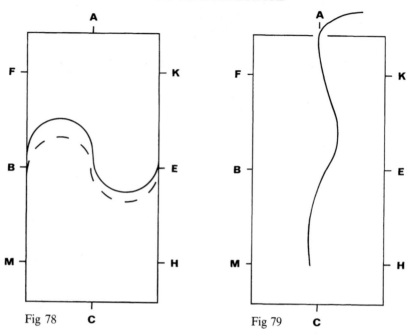

Fig 78   **C**   Fig 79   **C**

Glossary of Dressage Terms

Accepting the bit The willingness of the horse to accept the bit in his mouth and to respond to the aids without resistance.

Accepting the leg The willingness of the horse to accept the rider's leg against his side and respond without resistance to the rider's leg aids.

Accepting the weight The horse's willingness to carry the rider's weight without resistance.

Aids The signals that the rider sends to the horse through the legs, seat, hands and voice. These are supplemented by the artificial aids, the whip, spur and other schooling devices.

Balance In the horse, a relationship between speed and impulsion that results in the horse being able to respond to the rider's commands without delay or hesitation. In the rider, the ability to leave the body weight fully on the seat in the lowest part of the saddle, leaving legs, hands and arms free to apply the aids.

Bend The lateral bend throughout the length of the horse when making a turn or a circle.

Bit, above the Failing to accept the bit by lifting the head and the neck and resisting with the jaw.

Bit, behind the Failing to go forward onto the bit.

Cadence A spring in the step which enhances the rhythm and energy of the pace.

Canter A pace in three-time in which the feet come to the ground in the order: outside hind, inside hind and outside fore together, followed by the inside fore or leading leg. After a period of suspension, when none of the feet are on the ground, the stride is restarted with the outside hind.

Change of leg To change the leading leg in canter by a simple or flying change.

Change of rein To change the direction in the dressage arena.

Collection The lightening of the forehand by the engagement of the hip, stifle and hock joints, resulting in a lowering of the croup. The head is raised with the neck round and arched. The steps are shorter, rounder and more elevated than in the working paces.

Contact The feel kept in the rider's hand through the reins and bit to the horse's mouth.

Counter canter Cantering to the right with the left fore leading or vice versa.

Counter change of hand A zig-zag movement changing from half-pass right to half-pass left for a given number of steps and so on.

Diagonal To ride on a given pair of legs at rising trot, ie to lift the seat out of the saddle when one diagonal pair of feet come to the ground and lower it again when the next pair come to the ground.

Diagonal of the arena From 'F' to 'H', 'H' to 'F', 'K' to 'M' or 'M' to 'K' in the 20×40m arena.

Disunited An incorrect sequence of footfalls at canter when the pair of feet that come to the ground together are on the same side of the horse and not a diagonal pair.

Extension Taking the longest possible steps at any pace without loss of tempo, rhythm, balance or submission.

Falling-in Cutting the corners by bending the neck out and dropping the inside shoulder inwards.

Flexion The controlled bending of the neck to the left or the right.

Half-halt A rebalancing exercise in which the rider checks the speed with the fingers of the outside hand whilst maintaining or increasing the impulsion with the inside leg.

Half-pass A lateral movement in which the horse moves forwards and sideways at the same time bent in the direction in which he is going.

Half-pirouette Made at walk, canter or piaffer, this is a turn through 180° where the hind feet remain almost on the spot and the forefeet move through half a circle. The correct rhythm and tempo of the pace must be maintained.

Halt The horse stands square and immobile but balanced

and attentive ready to move forwards or backwards at the rider's command.

Hocks, engagement of the Flexing the hock joint to bring the hind legs further under the horse, thereby lowering the croup, lightening the forehand and increasing the impulsion.

Impulsion Controlled energy.

Lateral movements A term covering work in which the horse moves forwards and sideways at the same time. It can be done in all three paces. It includes the turn on the forehand, leg yielding, shoulder-in, travers, renvers and half-pass.

Pirouette A movement made in walk, canter or piaffer in which the horse makes a complete circle. The hind feet, almost marking time, make a very small circle and the forefeet make a circle the radius of which is the distance between the forefeet and the hind feet.

Renvers Similar to travers but the quarters are to the wall and the forehand taken off the track. The horse, looking in the direction in which he is going, is at about 40 to the wall.

Travers This is half-pass along the wall. The horse's forefeet continue straight along the track but the quarters are taken in off the track so that he is working clearly on three tracks.

Index